Ethics, Law and Natural Hazards

This book argues that the international community has a moral duty to intervene on behalf of a population affected by a natural hazard when their government is either unable or unwilling to provide basic, life-saving assistance.

The work draws on law, international relations theory, and political philosophy to articulate that non-response to a natural hazard is unethical. In providing policy suggestions, the author articulates what should happen based on an ethical analysis. Readers will thus gain an ethical lens with which to view intervention in the aftermath of a natural hazard. The book encourages readers to consider the nuances of arguments from various disciplines about whether or not an intervent is appropriate. Whilst arguing throughout that an intervention policy in response to natural hazards should be developed by the international community, the study also accounts for why intervention should only be used in very limited situations.

This interdisciplinary approach makes the book essential reading for researchers, academics and policymakers working in the areas of international law, humanitarian studies, human rights, international relations and political science.

Lauren Traczykowski teaches applied ethics in the Law School at Aston University, UK. Her research interests are in the areas of Applied Ethics and Emergency Situations.

Ethics, Law and Natural Hazards

The Moral Imperative for International Intervention Post-Disaster

Lauren Traczykowski

Routledge
Taylor & Francis Group
LONDON AND NEW YORK

First published 2021
by Routledge
2 Park Square, Milton Park, Abingdon, Oxon OX14 4RN

and by Routledge
52 Vanderbilt Avenue, New York, NY 10017

Routledge is an imprint of the Taylor & Francis Group, an informa business

British Library Cataloguing-in-Publication Data
A catalogue record for this book is available from the British Library

Library of Congress Cataloging-in-Publication Data
A catalog record has been requested for this book

ISBN: 978-0-367-40704-9 (hbk)

ISBN: 978-0-367-40912-8 (pbk)

ISBN: 978-0-367-80860-0 (ebk)

Typeset in Galliard
by Deanta Global Publishing Services, Chennai, India

TO
Dan, Chloe, Maya, Abby, Erin & Kenny
We have a responsibility to future generations.

Contents

Acknowledgements

My thanks and gratitude are owed to the following people: my reviewers for helpful comments and suggestions; the editorial staff at Routledge; the academics and staff of the School of Philosophy, Theology and Religion at the University of Birmingham, particularly Dr Jeremy Kidwell, Dr Jussie Suikkanen and Professor Heather Widdows; the academics and staff of Aston Law School at Aston University, specifically Dr Daniel Cash, Professor Simon Cooper, Mr Robert Goddard, Mrs Claire Howell, Mr Abhilash Nair, the late Professor Jill Poole, Dr Gayatri Patel and Dr Kristi Thomas for comments, guidance and support; and Dr Julian Lamb (Aston University) and Dr Ryan Murphy (Swansea University). Dr Peter West-Oram (Brighton and Sussex Medical School), Dr Chandrachur Singh (Miranda House, University of Delhi) and Dr Andrew Woodhall for comments and unwavering confidence. I owe my sanity to Dr Herjeet Marway, Dr Janice Baughan, and Mrs Shirit Bradley, and to Mr Joe Picciano, Ms Sonja Nieuwejaar and Mrs Penny Satches-Brohs for inspiring my love of the subject; Mr Daniel Hebert for checking my British; my family, for roots and wings. And Tim, for being everything I've needed. Thank you for nagging me to finish this book. You will never know how much I appreciate your unwavering love.

To everyone else who has travelled with me, thank you.

All errors and mistakes are my own.

1 The ethical gap

Reconciling intervention for natural hazards

Let us imagine that a national government is unable to provide adequate assistance in the aftermath of a natural hazard such as a hurricane, tsunami, earthquake and so on. Perhaps this is because they are unprepared for that particular type of event. Possibly it is because the government officials have themselves been killed or incapacitated by the emergency. It is plausible that the national government refuses to provide assistance to those affected within the country's borders. Perhaps, in this case, the government does not see the real impact. Alternatively, a corrupt regime could be uninterested in helping a particular group affected by the hazard.

Current global norms and international regulations on the matter suggest that international relief providers may offer assistance (IFRC, 2007). However, the receiving states must consent to such assistance, and "donor" states are forbidden from forcefully interfering (Multinational, 2007; O'Donnell, 2016; United Nations, 2016). Such non-consensual interventions, it is argued, run counter to the goal of international peace inherent in the international agreements on international disaster relief and recovery (IFRC, 2007). Instead, national governments and international organisations should try to persuade the affected governments or those we can identify as having some level of authority within the country to accept offers of assistance.

It is reasonable to assume that an individual would hope for someone to help if life-saving or life-sustaining support was not forthcoming in the aftermath of a natural hazard. Therefore, I start from the position that we would all want to be provided with assistance post-natural hazard should we need it. Indeed, we should all be able to make a claim for assistance should the need arise. I will argue that those affected by natural hazards are no less deserving of assistance than those affected by other emergencies. For this reason, we should develop international policies for intervention and the use of military force to provide assistance (in very specific and rare cases) when a national government is either unable or unwilling to provide assistance to its people in the aftermath of a large-scale natural hazard, even without consent from the affected government, based on our human right to welfare.

1.1 Hazards and disasters

We may all think that we know what a natural hazard is (an earthquake, a hurricane, etc.). However, this does not mean that we have an easy time explaining when a simple natural hazard triggers or becomes a disaster situation. Often we simply know what counts as a disaster based on our own previous experiences. Disasters exist at the intersection of social, ecological, political and economic situations and some trigger event. War, conflict, gas explosions and building fires can all represent types of disasters. In this book, my focus is on natural hazards as the trigger event. Just as a disaster need not flow from a natural hazard, a natural hazard may not result in a disaster (UNISDR, 2017). For this study, though, I am particularly interested in the disasters that occur in the immediate aftermath of a critical natural hazard.

Sudden onset, high-intensity natural hazards are the focus of this analysis. A natural hazard, just like the dropping of a bomb or chemical attack, is a complex but specific incident which requires a specific response. Whilst complex emergencies such as famine, climate change and poverty are destructive, they are not the type of emergency which requires or normally triggers immediate, proportionate response as argued for in this book.[1] Events that are commonly understood to be natural hazards include avalanches, earthquakes, floods, hurricanes, lightning, tornadoes, tsunamis, volcanic eruptions and wildfires (National Geographic, 2015). This is not an exhaustive list by any means. To this list, I would add drought, hailstorms, snowstorms and possibly solar storms, among others (FEMA, 2013).[2]

A disaster occurring in the aftermath of a natural hazard will disrupt the normal functioning of society and "involves great harm to a large number of people" (Zack, 2011, p. 2; IFRC, 2007). Hence, while a disaster usually involves the destruction of property and casualties, it need not result in death. Disasters involve a hazard, existing vulnerabilities and the limited ability of those in authority to respond to the event (National Disaster Coordinating Council (Phillippines), 2010). Often occurring after a hazard, disasters in themselves are slow-onset; to focus only on the hazard would be to misunderstand the disaster situation (Kelman, 2019). Disasters are multi-layered, multi-faceted outcomes of societal problems; they are the after-effect of any number of intersecting issues – economic, social, cultural, technological or environmental – and vulnerabilities (Kelman, 2008, 2019). In this way, disasters are dynamic and, as explained by the Sendai Framework for Disaster Risk Reduction, often result from poor risk management from state agencies in coordination with relevant stakeholders (UNISDR, 2015). Ultimately, disasters create chaos: they harm the health and well-being of people in a given society (Quarantelli & Dynes, 1973). Harm to the health of people and property are therefore central components of a disaster.[3]

Meanwhile, Dynes suggests that there are four ways of understanding a disaster: "the physical agent [i.e. the natural hazard], the physical consequences of the agent, the way in which the impact of the physical agent is evaluated and the social disruption and social changes brought about by the physical agent and its impact" (cited in Quarantelli & Dynes, 1977). Here Dynes claims that the physical event's impact on society is key to defining disaster. Still, Quarantelli notes that the background and experiences of the person describing the "disaster" will drastically impact how a disaster is defined (1998, p. 242). So, while a disaster has recognisable features and measurable impact, it is not simply the impact which characterises a disaster.

Interestingly, even if these are not temporal or quantifiable explanations of disasters, disasters are still always situated in a specific time and place (Convery et al., 2008, pp. 6–7; Neal, 1997, p. 259). Note that this does not include the size of the natural phenomenon, nor does it include the number of people affected. This is consistent with Neal's suggestion that disasters are best understood qualitatively and not temporally or quantitatively (1997). And so, for the purpose of this analysis, I take from these characterisations of the term that a disaster is the impact of a physical event on society in a harmful yet indeterminate way.

Importantly, disasters in the aftermath of a natural hazard trigger are sometimes irrevocably and causally linked with human factors. For example, anthropogenic climate change has been linked to an increase in ocean temperatures (NASA, 2020). Warmer oceans may be linked to stronger hurricanes (Category 4 or 5), which are more destructive (Buis, 2020). Then, vulnerability (including poverty), under-development and corruption can contribute to a process by which a natural hazard becomes a disaster (Lewis, 2010; Blaikie et al., 2003). Hence the idea that "natural disasters" are "natural" is a fallacy.

The disasters studied herein are "a combination of hazard and vulnerability" but, importantly, with a specific focus on natural hazards (Kelman et al., 2016). This combination and intersection of meteorological events, hazards, vulnerability and situations is absent from philosophical enquiry and political planning. However, a philosophical approach to disaster response in the aftermath of a natural hazard will help us investigate our duties and responsibilities with this type of trigger.

In addition, humanitarian intervention literature (and associated policies) purposely removes "natural disasters" – defined as earthquakes, volcanoes, etc., so "natural hazards" – from its focus, suggesting that they are separate emergency types (Wheeler, 2010; Archibugi, 2004). Indeed, the intervention literature (separate from the development and relief literature) does not engage with natural hazards and discuss how to respond or intervene after a tsunami or earthquake whether we consider those hazards to be natural or human-influenced anyway, even if the underlying societal and environmental vulnerabilities are the same.

Hence, I am interested specifically in "natural hazards" because they are excluded from the relevant literature and from international policy. If we want to talk about the social construction, resilience to natural hazards and the problems that different groups will have towards becoming resilient, we must first put disasters resulting from natural hazards into the appropriate literature.

1.2 Scope

Whilst not quantitatively or temporally definitive, I focus my analysis on a particular type of post-natural hazard disaster. Consider the following. In 2014,

Chile experienced a series of earthquakes which killed six people. According to official reports, close to a million people were displaced due to the threat of a resultant tsunami (RT, 2015). This would qualify as a disaster triggered by a natural hazard under my use of the term. This is because, whilst there were not a high number of fatalities, the earthquake created a huge disruption to society: escaped prisoners had to be re-apprehended; special forces had to be called in to guard supermarkets and private homes from looters; and adobe houses in rural communities unable to withstand the earthquake crumbled, causing death and homelessness (Franklin, 2014).

There are often earthquakes which cause the ground to rumble, make people dizzy and disrupt the normal daily routine. Whilst still a natural hazard, these earthquakes would not qualify as disasters under my use of the term. You will note that I accept that an event can trigger a disaster even when there is a low fatality rate. However, simply making a lot of people uncomfortable is not sufficient to qualify a trigger event and its consequences as a disaster. The point here is not to offer a number of affected people which qualifies an event as a disaster, but rather to show that the natural hazard's impact event must be large in scale and severe in at least some aspects.

Military intervention for the purpose of natural hazard disaster support is legally prohibited by the United Nations Charter (United Nations, 2015). Chapter VII of the UN Charter establishes that force can only be used in situations that constitute a threat to international peace. Furthermore, intervention into the domestic affairs of another state (disaster response is considered a domestic affair) is likewise prohibited by Article 2(7) of the UN Charter (Massingham, 2009, p. 812). Still further, the Responsibility to Protect (RtoP), as adopted by the UN at the 2005 World Summit, excludes intervention in the aftermath of a natural hazard (ICISS, 2001; UN General Assembly, 2005).[4]

Discussions of whether we should intervene militarily after a natural hazard first occurred during the development of the RtoP (see Chapter 6) and then were re-energised when Cyclone Nargis hit Myanmar in 2008 (see Chapters 5 and 6) (Bowley & Erlanger, 2008; Evans, 2008). Without a standing policy, I expect that a large-scale disaster which resembles the emergency in Burma will trigger a second debate on the topic in the future.

Notably, a natural hazard intervention norm which accounts for the stipulations of the UN Charter yet allows for intervention – like the norm of RtoP – does not exist.[5] Instead, the rules outlined by the UN Charter set a precedent and deter any interventions of the kind that I suggest in this book. My hope is that my argument for the development of a natural hazard intervention policy, based specifically on the human right to welfare, adds to this debate and contributes to ethical solutions proposed so that a solution might be found before it is needed.

Considering the purposeful absence of natural hazards from legal intervention, this argument is contentious. Despite the likely rare use or necessity of the policy suggested herein, the central thesis should at least be considered when people are affected by a large-scale natural hazard. Furthermore, it should be discussed and prepared for well in advance of the policy's implementation.

I propose policy suggestions because a legal structure, based on the ethical requirement to allow intervention post-natural hazard, does not exist. Sovereignty (see Chapter 7), legal precedent and norms of international law (Chapter 3) stand in the way of a robust discussion from taking place, let alone a policy being developed.

I set out the scope of my argument here but recognise that, due to space constraints, I will not be able to discuss all elements. Additionally, I will not address harms directly caused by human actions or the disasters triggered by non-natural hazards.

First, then, I will not discuss harms that have been directly caused by human vulnerabilities or those disasters to which human activity has directly contributed to the occurrence (see Kelly, 2014). For example, the looting and police brutality that occurred in New Orleans after Hurricane Katrina contributed to the ongoing crisis situation. However, these are knock-on effects from official inaction in the aftermath of a natural hazard. Likewise, I will not comment on the poverty situation (an aspect of vulnerability) in Louisiana which contributed to citizens' inability to evacuate and hence the exacerbation of the disaster. My focus would instead be the government's poor response to the hurricane and their lack of direct support to those affected by that hurricane instead of their response to the looting or poverty, although I accept that they are related.[6]

Additionally, explicitly "human-made" disasters are purposely absent from my analysis because they are either directly caused by humans or influenced by human action, which leads to difficult debates about responsibility and compensation. Admittedly, there are instances where there is an overlap between "natural hazards" and "human-made" categories. However, for the purposes of this study, it is both possible and useful to make the distinction between natural hazards and purely man-made disasters and to focus on the former.

For example, as a consequence of the anthropogenic global warming, natural hazards – floods, hurricanes and so on – are now more frequent. The Intergovernmental Panel on Climate Change has noted that increased global temperatures contribute to changes in the likelihood of the occurrence and the strength of extreme weather (Intergovernmental Panel on Climate Change, 2013). However, climate-change-related disasters will not be discussed in my thesis because they are long-term issues with ample warning time for responders and policymakers.[7] The flood or hurricane and its impact on the lives and well-being of those affected will be discussed.

I also note that some disasters are too strongly linked to human-made factors to be adequately addressed by my suggested plans alone. For this reason, I do not intend to address situations like famines or oil spills either. Famine, while most often caused by drought, cannot be adequately addressed without considering food security, armed conflict, genetically modified alternative sources, global trade and the price of staple products. While such concerns are relevant and clearly exacerbate disasters triggered by natural hazards, it is impossible to address famine in the category discussed herein. Similarly, oil and chemical spills are caused by the pursuit, transport and use of crude oil and toxic chemicals.

Nuclear plant explosions and leaks result from human error in the pursuit of energy. These hazards are therefore too closely linked to human error to be analysed like the hurricanes, earthquakes, and so on of this research.

Also, responses to incidents that fall outside the category of natural hazard are very often accounted for in international policies. Norms of behaviour often dictate how countries should act to aid those in their countries who are affected by incidents categorised as emergencies or conflicts. I have thus narrowed the scope of my argument to focus solely on international response to natural hazards precisely because it falls outside existing norms and policies for how the international community should militarily respond.

Likewise, I am not suggesting that natural hazard response is a forgotten type of response. Globally, there are many reciprocal emergency response agreements in place which allow for consensual foreign emergency response (NATO, 1998; European Commission, 2011; Office of the Press Secretary, 2006). However, there is no mechanism for intervening in natural hazard scenarios when a national government cannot or will not consent to assistance. A non-consensual response with force is rejected by the international community for reasons discussed herein. I argue, though, that non-intervention is possibly damaging to the rights of those affected by a natural hazard and hence the international community must be proactive in developing policy which addresses state-level non-compliance.

1.3 Structure

My main conclusion will be that military intervention for the purpose of natural hazard response is ethically required in some situations in which a national government is unable or unwilling to provide assistance to those affected. To that end, the international community is morally obligated to create policies which guide national governments as to when and how military intervention in response to a natural hazard should be carried out, or so I will argue. My argument for these conclusions will proceed with the following structure.

In Chapter 2, I engage with the theory underpinning my central argument. I give an overview of disaster studies, humanitarian intervention and cosmopolitan literatures as they pertain to that argument. In doing so, I explain the gap left at the overlap of these literatures, which needs rectification with a post-natural-hazard intervention policy.

In Chapter 3, I explain current international laws and regulations pertaining to international military interventions and how they do not account for the impact of natural hazards. Two major norms associated with international intervention are the RtoP and Just War Theory. Each is discussed in turn to set the scene for future possible approaches to intervene for a large-scale natural hazard response in Chapter 7. Likewise, there must be consideration of what it means to carry out a just intervention. In this chapter, I re-introduce natural hazards as a trigger for military intervention. I suggest that many of the same issues of justice would be present for military intervention after a natural hazard as would be present for human rights abuses or genocide.

In Chapter 4, I explain the human right to welfare from a philosophical perspective. I begin with an overview of human rights in general. I then proceed to a discussion of the human right to welfare and how it guarantees that all humans have a claim to a basic level of primary goods. Whilst there are three possible ways to ground this right – in the badness of pain and suffering, in our interaction with others or in the recognition of our joint humanity – I make the case that the humanity-based grounding is the most appropriate. Accordingly, the human right to welfare requires that the international community fulfils its duties associated with the right. I thus argue that the international community has an obligation to provide for the welfare of humans no matter their geographical location or, pertinent to this thesis, what emergency they face. This chapter thus offers the main justification for the development of policy for and the preparation to act on behalf of those humans affected by a natural hazard when a national government is unable or unwilling to provide for its people.

In Chapter 5, I provide a case study to help situate my argument in real world events. I explain and analyse the phases of disaster response in general before turning to discussion of Cyclone Nargis which hit Myanmar (Burma) in 2008. The national government, for a period of time, refused international assistance as the domestic population suffered.

In Chapter 6, I start to formulate my main argument, setting out the current laws and standards as they relate to natural hazard intervention. I then explain the problems associated with maintaining the status quo of intervention. I set out my justification for why (and when) we should intervene in the aftermath of a natural hazard, arguing that there are some cases in which such interventions are appropriate and even required. The main consequence of this is that existing international policies are inadequate. Accordingly, I argue that the human right to welfare may require the international community to intervene in certain cases.

In Chapter 7, I outline the basic principles for future natural hazard military intervention policies. I first explain preparedness measures which such policies will require. I then develop the basic principles of natural hazard intervention policies on the basis of Just War Theory. Like any military intervention policy, an ethical natural hazard intervention policy will require that military interventions in natural hazard scenarios will have a just cause and they must be proportional last resort responses, based on the right authority. Due consideration must also be made for the long-term consequences and the main objections of such an intervention policy.

Chapter 8 addresses the weightiest objection to my policy proposal: sovereign authority over a territory. In arguing against sovereignty as a barrier to natural hazard intervention, I begin with what sovereignty is and why it is valued in international society. I then set out the main sovereignty-based objections to my thesis before explaining that sovereignty is not a moral barrier to the provision of assistance through military force. Interventions may support the re-establishment of sovereign governments and uphold the sovereign rights of the individuals within the affected country.

In sum, I argue that those affected by a natural hazard are no less worthy of assistance from the international community than are those who are affected by gross human rights abuses or genocide. The new international policy outlined will, at a minimum, contribute to future discussion by the international community. Most importantly, though, the development of a natural hazard military intervention policy will ensure that we are prepared to carry out our duties associated with the human right to welfare. Indeed, by creating a policy for interventions in natural hazard scenarios, we express equal moral concern for all human beings and act on our duty to help everyone in the aftermath of a natural hazard.

Notes

1 Slow-onset disasters are the outcome of a grouping of factors and can be even more disastrous than those with a specific trigger; however, these often require a developmental rather than an emergency response.
2 Some disasters may result from a natural hazard only (say, a solar storm) and will not depend on the "vulnerability" of the society it affects; sometimes, nothing can be done to avoid or create resiliency so as to diminish the impact of this kind of natural phenomenon (Kelman et al., 2016).
3 See legal definitions offered by the Tampere Convention, the International Law Commission and the International Disaster Response Law Guidelines.
4 See Chapter 6 for a full discussion of the current legal position on intervention for a natural hazard response. It should be noted that this is not intended as an exhaustive legal analysis. The goal is to provide an interdisciplinary applied ethics analysis to the legal status quo which shows that laws on natural hazard response and intervention require further ethical analysis, discussion and amendment.
5 Susan Breau asserts that "the obligations upon a state to ensure the survival of a population has to extend beyond armed conflict or civil unrest" and therefore argues for the inclusion of disasters as part of the RtoP. I do not argue for the disasters triggered by natural hazards to be included in the RtoP doctrine but do similarly argue that states have an obligation to support their people in this kind of scenario (2016, p. 73).
6 Intensive risk is the "risk associated to high-severity, mid to low-frequency events, mainly associated with major hazards"; extensive risks are "low-severity, high-frequency" events (PreventionWeb, 2015). I focus on intensive risks because I am interested in the response to the hazard in question instead of the factors which contributed to its development into a disaster. The issues of poverty and social vulnerabilities are rightly identified as contributing factors in the creation of disaster. For more on vulnerability and a lack of resilience as contributing factors in disasters, see Cutter et al. (2008) and Carter et al. (2007). The response to intensive risks are consistently understood as the responsibility of a national government (Tokunaga, 2014; IFRC, 2007).
7 While I will not discuss climate change, the resultant storms should be included as "natural hazards". Sudden-onset natural events pose a threat to human life no matter the cause.

2 Theoretical situation of natural hazard response

The argument made within this text is interdisciplinary in approach. I have positioned my argument at the overlap of three distinct areas of literature: disaster studies, humanitarian intervention (within the broader international relations discipline including aspects of international law) and cosmopolitanism (within the philosophical and global ethics disciplines). In Section 2.1, I engage with disaster studies including the agents of disaster, how natural hazard response has a distinct character amongst other types of response and may contain a military component, and finally the role of preparedness in natural hazard response. This discussion provides a base from which I can make a wider argument about how the policies I suggest are appropriate. In Section 2.2, I engage with humanitarian intervention – both the theory and practice – and how it has evolved from being statist to being driven by human rights norms. However, humanitarian interventions are not carried out for natural hazards; this is problematic and a gap in the intervention literature. Cosmopolitanism, as a political and ethical theory, gives us a helpful perspective in understanding the normative shift toward the primacy of human rights in humanitarian intervention as well as the requirements of disaster ethics. In Section 2.3, I therefore discuss cosmopolitanism as a theoretical approach to global policy and I show how grounding humanitarian intervention in state-based duties is inaccurate and unnecessary. I then make the case in Section 2.4 that at the overlap of disaster response, humanitarian intervention and cosmopolitanism, space exists to consider post-natural hazard intervention and the subsequent development of ethical policy.

2.1 Disaster studies and ethics

I begin here with the disaster response literature and the corresponding ethics which spans centuries and requires knowledge of an array of fields including geography, communications, logistics, and emergency medicine to name a few (O'Mathuna, 2014; Voltaire, 1918; Quarantelli, 1998, 2000; Quarantelli & Dynes, 1973; Alexander, 2015). There are three aspects of the response literature relevant to my argument. First, there is a distinction to be made between natural and other (i.e. human) agents of disasters.[1] Second, force is often used in natural hazard response and thus the use of force may be justified in certain circumstances. Third, preparedness plays an important role in disaster response. Using these aspects of disaster response I explain how disaster ethics should be applied to natural hazard scenarios.

First, on agents of disaster, I am specifically concerned with natural hazards and not other agents as the trigger for a disaster (as explained in Chapter 1). Quarantelli explains that such a differentiation does not change the degree to which humans prepare for and/or react to a given emergency (2000). However, international policies already do differentiate and specifically remove natural hazards (written as "natural disasters") from the list of possible reasons for the international community to take action. Indeed, the debates leading to the development and implementation of the Responsibility to Protect doctrine removed natural hazards [disasters] as a trigger because it was thought it would make the Responsibility to Protect doctrine too demanding, thus undermining international consensus and adoption (Thakur, 2008). (Likewise, in developing a cosmopolitan approach to humanitarian intervention, Archibugi explains that response to natural hazards is a separate type of response taken by national governments and without a military component (2004).)[2]

The second area of the disaster literature I address is the use of force. Even with civilian authorities remaining in charge, it is widely accepted that a military force may be called upon when "it appears that civilian resources will be inadequate" (Anderson, n.d., p. 417). Indeed, military participation in a natural hazard response is far from abnormal. Sometimes it is vital to the integration of specialist personnel, equipment and logistical support (Anderson, n.d.).

In fact, many emergency management agencies had their origins in civil defence. Military-style resources and staff have been used in both civilian and military operations (Quarantelli, 2000). This tradition continues with Civil Defense forces in Russia (EMERCOM), Italy (Civil Protection Department) and National Guard troops in the US, among others, who are called up to respond to civilian emergencies (EMERCOM of Russia, 2017; Protezione Civile, 2017; Soucy, 2012; Stuhltrager, 2006). It is therefore logical to suggest that military force may be necessary to provide assistance and stabilise a region in the aftermath of a natural hazard as I argue in Section 5.2 and Chapter 6.

Furthermore, military control over a particular emergency (in non-military led democracies, at least), is rarely implemented and then only under severe circumstances (Stuhltrager, 2006; Matthews, n.d.). However, there has been a growing trend toward extended use of such assets in natural hazard response and the structures are in place to call upon domestic militaries should they become necessary (Bawden, 2014; Hofmann & Hudson, 2009). I am not suggesting that possible military control over natural hazard responses should be the default response. Instead, we must recognise that using military forces in natural hazard response is common.

Finally, so as to maintain the balance of civilian over military response, there is a need for proper preparedness. Emergency planning involves systematically preparing for an unknown future disaster (Alexander, 2015). Realistically, not all humans can be saved in a disaster (Zack, 2011). Likewise, different countries respond to disasters in different ways and some may not have the capacity to respond appropriately. Walzer goes so far as to suggest that the circumstances of "supreme emergencies" may require that normal rules of practice be overridden or suspended (2004).

Instead, I contend that proper preparedness which keeps us in line with our peacetime ethics and which will help save the maximum number of people is possible. Indeed, I argue with Zack that disaster ethics – how we treat and support the individuals affected – should not be situation dependent (2011, p. xiv). We should not consider setting aside our ethics in emergency situations. If we follow Zack's approach to *Disaster Ethics* instead of Walzer's *Emergency Ethics* there should not be a need to suspend our morals when faced with a crisis (Zack, 2011; Walzer, 2004). With the best preparation possible, as Zack suggests, our day-to-day focus on individual human rights should be enforceable on a larger and more urgent scale (2011). This point by Zack is one of the reasons I make a strong case for international preparedness in the event that a national government is unable or unwilling to assist its own people after a natural hazard.

Zack's insight into disaster ethics comes from her recognition that a triage approach to disaster response (because of its prioritisation of certain individuals over others) is insufficient. Hence whilst she supports the utilitarian adage of Save the Greatest Number, she provides a caveat which suggests a move away from a purely utilitarian approach to emergency situations (Zack, 2011). Carrying out the greatest preparation possible will necessarily involve the recognition that states may not have available resources and plans may go wrong or be ignored; this does not justify poor assistance offered to those affected by a disaster.

I contend that her move away from traditional approaches to disaster ethics provides space for a cosmopolitan approach to disaster ethics and provides a way to focus on the individuals affected. In this way, disaster ethics is (or should be) cosmopolitan in nature. My argument is thereby positioned in the middle ground: between cosmopolitan justice for those suffering the effects of a natural hazard and the realistic expectation of how many people can be saved and assisted, given the circumstances at the time.

Hence, a well-prepared disaster plan may save the greatest number but, more importantly, will also ensure that the saving of each individual is accounted for in those plans. (I explain in Chapter 3 how we should prioritise individual rights over state rights and the importance of saving humans because of their inherent moral worth (Pogge, 1992; Caney, 2010).) In order to be consistent with a cosmopolitan approach to disaster response, as I argue for, when a national government is unable or unwilling to provide assistance to its own people, I provide an ethical justification for natural hazard intervention in this study.

2.2 Humanitarian intervention

Before moving to the overlap between disaster studies and cosmopolitanism, I first discuss humanitarian intervention. The humanitarian intervention literature already benefits from the application of cosmopolitan theory and is the closest established field of study to the type of intervention I argue for herein. I include the humanitarian intervention literature as a way of showing what international policies and norms exist currently and hence what is possible for post-natural hazard intervention. Thus I first note the reasons given in the literature for carrying out a humanitarian intervention, namely international stability and individual rights, so that I can make a full argument on justifiable reasons for intervention in Chapters 6 and 7. Having explained the ethics which have historically underpinned humanitarian intervention (which I link to Walzer most notably) as well as the ethics which currently ground humanitarian intervention (which I attribute in main part to Wheeler) I move towards explaining what ethics *should* drive interventions argued for herein.

I begin with two prominent reasons for carrying out humanitarian interventions: international stability and, more recently, human rights (Section 4.2). Michael Walzer provides a thorough explanation of the perils of humanitarian intervention and affirms the need for justifying any intervention. He explains that interventions will likely result in additional suffering or disturbance to the peace and well-being of a given territory. Foreign armies should thus be prohibited from intervening in any country because of the special relationship between citizen and state and the benefits individuals receive as a result of this relationship (Walzer, 1980). (These benefits can be understood as the benefits of sovereignty (Section 8.2).)

Walzer argues that the reason for carrying out an intervention should primarily be to restore or protect international stability and thus asserts the primacy of internationalism. By this he means maintenance of the international state system and the need for peace and security within it. Indeed, he argues that interventions should be carried out only as exceptions to the normal rules of sovereignty (Walzer, 2006, pp. 90–91). Intervention to stem the advance of violence from one country to the region and the world may therefore be justified (Walzer, 1995).

Our obligations to other humans are then secondary, supportive reasons for an intervention justified on the grounds of international stability, according to Walzer (1995). On this, the traditional view of what a moral justification for humanitarian intervention would look like, it could be argued that only genocide may be a strong enough reason to intervene. Indeed, when suffering is extreme and "shocks the conscience" of humanity, an intervention may be necessary (Walzer, 1995).[3] According to Walzer this blend of practical and moral reasons for intervention is necessary because "pure moral will doesn't exist in political life" (2002, p. 5). Hence the practical reasons for intervening must be considered first before we will be able to garner enough support for an intervention based on moral reasons.[4]

I agree that intervention should be an exception to normal practice and not our go-to method of stopping injustice (Walzer, 2006, p. 91). Furthermore, we cannot intervene for all human rights abuses as the number of instances where that would be required would be too demanding. Still further, intervention is not sufficiently justified based on the fact that domestic sources cannot end the abuse and suffering quickly (Walzer, 2002). We must be careful and considered about how and when we intervene.

However, I take issue with the moral foundations of Walzer's argument. Speaking of practicalities before moral imperatives undermines the value of humanity in general. Likewise, I am interested in the moral component of state legitimacy and not the political recognition of "legitimate" governments. Whilst a *human*itarian intervention should be about upholding *human* rights, Walzer gives more practical reasons for intervention which seem to overshadow and guide decision making.

Furthermore, David Luban explains that we cannot support interventions strictly into states that are illegitimate (1980). As is discussed in Chapter 7, even legitimate states (which have rights to non-intervention) may experience a disaster that renders them unable to support the needs of their citizens. Indeed, legitimate states may exacerbate the suffering of their own people and still be considered politically legitimate.

Additionally, Walzer's view on sovereignty has been heavily criticised for putting states' rights, or the rights of individuals within particular state-citizen relationships, above the rights of individuals in general (Doppelt, 1978; Luban, 1980). Cabrera further criticises Walzer's support of sovereignty as it inhibits the development of a robust global adoption of human rights norms (which puts Walzer at odds with the cosmopolitan ideal) (2010). Walzer accepts that even he cannot consistently uphold sovereignty as absolute considering the "arbitrary and accidental character of state boundaries" (2006, p. 89). He has recognised that imposed suffering may come from internal sources stemming from state failure or embedded structural hatred and inequalities (Walzer, 1995). This supports the argument I make in Section 8.4 that sovereignty need not be the barrier to natural hazard intervention it is often said to be.

Walzer's justifications for non-intervention stood as a norm in international relations for decades and still play a significant role in diplomatic conversations about future interventions.[5] However, in line with a shift away from the supremacy of states (see Chapter 7) and toward a human rights norm within international relations (see Chapter 3), there is an increasingly recognised imperative to act on behalf of the human rights of others. Indeed, Nicholas Wheeler's book *Saving Strangers* offered international relations theorists and practitioners a practical view on the shifting norm within humanitarian intervention (Wheeler, 2010). Importantly, Wheeler argues for the primacy of international law based on shared norms. International law can and does create binding obligations on states because of these shared norms and thereby has legitimate authority (Wheeler, 2010).

For the most part, Wheeler endorses the Responsibility to Protect (RtoP) and its case for intervention in scenarios where governments are committing genocide, large-scale human rights abuses, humanitarian emergencies and ethnic cleansing (Wheeler, 2005). He explains that RtoP's adoption moved the intervention discussion from debates about a government's sovereignty, to the international community's responsibilities to individuals (Wheeler, 2005). This shift demonstrates the more general normative trend which prioritises human rights over sovereignty. Increasingly, human rights violations are seen as an appropriate justification for intervention (Beitz, 2001; Donnelly, 2014; Ignatieff, 2000). It is also crucial to my argument and my rejection of sovereignty as a reason to avoid intervention when people are suffering in the aftermath of a natural hazard.

In justifying humanitarian intervention, Wheeler, like Walzer, utilises the Just War tradition and sets out criteria which must be met in order to justly engage in a humanitarian intervention. Important for this discussion is his specification of a "supreme humanitarian emergency" as a just cause for intervention (Wheeler, 2010, p. 33). He explains that setting the parameters for what qualifies as a supreme humanitarian emergency is "too arbitrary" to be effective; instead, such an emergency is one in which the only hope of survival is being rescued by those outside our political community – namely foreigners (Wheeler, 2010, p. 34).

Wheeler's justification for "saving strangers" in humanitarian emergencies thereby supports my argument for intervening when a natural hazard causes extreme risk to life and a national government is not helping its own people to survive (Chapter 6). However, the RtoP doctrine does not account for natural hazards (see Section 2.2.3). "Natural disasters" were purposefully excluded because broad consensus for RtoP's adoption could not be reached if it was too broad and was too demanding on interveners (Thakur, 2008). Considering it is not included in the list of triggers for humanitarian intervention, I aim to explain that the suffering of those affected by a natural hazard is not morally different from the suffering of those experiencing genocide, war crimes, ethnic cleansing and crimes against humanity, which will trigger a RtoP response and hence "deserves" intervention. In doing this, I work within the overlap of the disaster and humanitarian intervention literature. As natural hazards are not included, I press beyond RtoP and show why a cosmopolitan approach to natural hazard intervention is more appropriate.

A complementary approach to humanitarian intervention, also grounded in cosmopolitan perspectives will move us to a full adoption of the human rights norms required for natural hazard response. Archibugi defines cosmopolitan humanitarian intervention thus: "A military intervention in an area for the purpose of saving peoples from democide or other major violations of human rights occurring and carried out by foreign institutions without the consent of a legitimate government" (2003, p. 3). He goes on to argue that intervention purposefully excludes action taken in the aftermath of a natural hazard which he says is carried out by national governments and without a military component (Archibugi, 2004). Archibugi's analysis and explanation of cosmopolitan humanitarian intervention is robust and a necessary contribution to the literature on both intervention and cosmopolitanism and thus is the correct place to analyse an overlap between natural hazard response, humanitarian intervention and cosmopolitanism. However, Archibugi's assumption that natural hazards should be excluded from cosmopolitan intervention policy requires redress.

Archibugi also suggests that offers of assistance in the aftermath of natural hazards are indeed often consented to by the affected government (2004). However, there are instances in which national governments do not or will not accept foreign assistance. The Burmese government's refusal of assistance (Section 5.2) is a prime example of a government's inability or unwillingness to accept foreign assistance. As Archibugi himself argues,"… humanitarian intervention is too precious a concept to be decided on the hoof or, worse still, invoked to mask special interests or designs on power" (2003, p. 10). Hence we must take account of and prepare for the development of intervention frameworks which are not decided on whims or to mask power plays. I establish such a framework in Chapter 7.

Interventions are often seen as smokescreens for imperialist intentions (see Section 6.3.1). Archibugi argues that the development of cosmopolitan institutions, as argued for by institutional cosmopolitans (Section 5.3.2), will firmly establish the development of norms and procedures around the needs of individuals and not states (2004). The adoption of institutional cosmopolitanism will also contribute to the effectiveness of military interventions in general. This will move humanitarian intervention from the realm of statist, imperialist politics to that of individual, cosmopolitan politics, focused on human rights. Such changes to global institutions will re-focus our endeavours on human individuals and will ensure that authority is carried out for the right reasons and with the right authority in the aftermath of a natural hazard.

2.3 Cosmopolitanism

I have thus far explained the disaster studies and humanitarian intervention literatures and how they relate to my thesis. In line with the cosmopolitan tradition of developing and implementing a moral ideal, I have included cosmopolitan approaches to disaster studies and humanitarian intervention to demonstrate a link between distinct literatures. Use of a cosmopolitan approach is also helpful in setting out the ethical position taken throughout this text. In this section, I first explain why cosmopolitanism is the approach I use and then how it supports the dovetailing of the other two literatures.

Luis Cabrera has argued that a cosmopolitan view of global politics, and global citizenship in particular, will help us recognise all humans as "co-equal agents … justified in pressing their own interests" (2010, p. 14). Indeed, even the weakest form of cosmopolitanism assumes the equal moral worth of all humans (Miller, 2005; Pogge, 2002). A cosmopolitan viewpoint will move us away from the common view that those in developing countries are in some way "passive recipients of morally required transfers" (2010, p. 14). If we follow Cabrera's argument and view all humans as active participants in their own future, the idea that anyone is a "victim", and in some way worthy only of our pity instead of our compassion, falls away.

Humans affected by natural hazards are not "victims". We experience and suffer through and from events; we do not become passive recipients, incapable of claiming the goods associated with human rights. In this way, we do not donate to those affected out of some moral duty to support the less fortunate (Cabrera, 2010, p. 19). We should provide assistance (donation or otherwise) because humans continue to claim the goods associated with basic human rights regardless of the emergency they face. In Sections 4.1 and 4.2, I explain how the human right to a basic minimum of certain necessary goods is of the highest priority for society and how it must be universal in application. Fulfilment of negative duties to ensure the basic survival needs of compatriots or foreigners are met is consistent with global justice supported by most forms of cosmopolitanism (intermediate and strong at least) (Pogge, 2002). Accordingly, all humans can claim the goods associated with the human right to welfare in a natural hazard scenario.

Following from this, Cabrera makes the argument that we should direct our energies at individuals as the morally significant entity. This is a move away from statist accounts of moral obligation. Instead, any institutions grounded in the statist system should be used for the promotion of human rights. It is the human aspect of human rights themselves, not the pain and suffering or interdependence between states, that create the duties to humans (Cabrera, 2010, p. 33). This further supports the notion that states are neither responsible for humans because of some duty to help those less fortunate, nor as part of a mutual assistance compact. Indeed, sovereignty must take a back seat to a state's duties to support the needs of individuals purely because humans are inherently valuable (Cabrera, 2010).

In arguing against the prioritisation of compatriots over those humans living in other countries, Cabrera argues that the possibility of oppression and an inability for governments to meet the needs of their people should encourage us to look more closely at rights-based approaches to global justice (Cabrera, 2004). In fact, if the building of cosmopolitan institutions will ensure certain necessary (subsistence) goods are available to individuals, then we are morally required to develop those institutions (Cabrera, 2010).

Cabrera's interpretation of the cosmopolitan ideal is arguably overextended. He sets out a position in which the norm of human rights must be established within an ideal version of a global institutional structure. Whilst admirable, it is arguably impractical in the short term and questionably undesirable in the long term (Das, 2006). Full development of cosmopolitan global institutions is unnecessary in order to establish policies in line with human rights norms. Instead, the recognition of our negative duties to other humans to ensure basic means of survival is sufficiently cosmopolitan and just to make the argument within this book (Pogge, 1992). Considering the world exists in non-ideal conditions of justice (and is unlikely to reach ideal conditions any time soon), there are ways of functioning within our current unjust systems whilst pursuing cosmopolitan goals (Freiman, 2013).

2.4 The overlap

Let us therefore apply a cosmopolitan approach (like the one applied to humanitarian intervention) to human rights in natural hazard scenarios. Cosmopolitanism helps us to understand that there are just some phenomena over which a state cannot govern. In arguing for cosmopolitan democracy, Archibugi suggests that we must not just set out the ideal cosmopolitan solution to global problems. The full realisation of human rights requires that we develop new and innovative ways of approaching global affairs which account for the needs of all individuals globally (Archibugi, 2003, p. 8). Hence we must innovatively apply cosmopolitan ideals on the global stage separate from the statist system (Archibugi, 2003, p. 7).

Importantly, he notes that whilst the human rights of certain individuals may be violated in various circumstances, humanitarian interventions should only occur when "blatant, collective violations of human rights are perpetrated" (Archibugi, 2004, p. 6). Explaining the grounds for cosmopolitan humanitarian interventions in this way actually sets Archibugi in line with Walzer in that some human rights may be violated should the emergency require it. As explained above, I do not believe we should ever establish that violating human rights may be justified. Instead, with proper preparation in the face of large-scale natural hazards, we may be able to change the institutions and systems through which disaster assistance is delivered. This requires proper preparedness to include a provision for the use of force when a national government is unable or unwilling to provide for the needs of its people in the aftermath of a natural hazard, or so I argue.[6]

Thus, in what follows I work at the overlap of disaster response, humanitarian intervention, and cosmopolitanism. The ethics of disaster response herein are underpinned by cosmopolitan ethics. Disaster response requires the development of just policies developed with the prioritisation of human individuals within those policies. However, the ethics of disaster response, as I apply it, relies on norms and structures already developed in the humanitarian intervention literature. Indeed, any of the problems faced by humanitarian intervention academics will be problems I face as well. In establishing the ethical grounds for and the specifics of a natural hazard intervention policy, I reject the exclusion of natural hazards from the disaster studies, cosmopolitan and humanitarian intervention literature and bring natural hazards into the fold of ethical theorising and policy development.

Notes

1 For more, see (Blaikie et al., 2003).
2 It is appropriate for me to differentiate between natural and other agents of disaster to show that there is a gap in the humanitarian, cosmopolitan, and philosophy literature as well as in relevant international policies.
3 Any intervention must take into account the impact such an act will have on those doing the intervention and those in the country being intervened (Walzer, 2002).
4 A pure moral will is unlikely to garner enough support to maintain the intervention and accept casualties that will likely occur (Walzer, 2002, p. 6).
5 His later works provide evidence, however, that the use of force should be seen as a commitment to others to save them from suffering (Walzer, 2002).
6 Please note that I am suggesting a "*provision* for the use of force" in the named circumstances. I am not suggesting that the use of force becomes the status quo or is utilised frequently.

3 International laws and norms for intervention in the context of natural hazards

Current international laws and doctrines do not allow for an international intervention when a domestic government is unable or unwilling to respond to a natural hazard within its own borders. Consequently, policies and procedures for such intervention have not been developed. Any assistance to a population affected by a natural hazard is the responsibility of a domestic government and aid, particularly when military support is involved, should only be deployed "with the express consent of the affected State" (IFRC, 2007). This means that those affected by a natural hazard (as opposed to conflict, war or humanitarian emergency) are extremely vulnerable (see discussion in Section 2.1). Reliance on a national government to respond and the associated lack of policy, laws and doctrines at the international level can put those affected by a natural hazard at a high risk of mortality and morbidity.

The absence of laws is the challenge and the opportunity to which I now turn. In this chapter, I consider the existing international laws and norms for interventions as they currently stand. I focus mainly on Article VII of the UN Charter and the Responsibility to Protect Doctrine. This chapter thus provides the background for my argument for intervention policy in natural hazard scenarios in Chapter 6.

In Section 3.1, I provide context to and make a distinction between intervention, just intervention and disaster relief. In Section 3.2.1, I provide an account of intervention policies and norms as they currently exist. Having done so, I then discuss two major normative approaches to intervention: Just War Theory (3.2.2) and the Responsibility to Protect (3.2.3). In discussing Just War Theory I provide one way of understanding when it is just/appropriate to intervene into the affairs of another state. Similarly, I describe the relevant components of the Responsibility to Protect (RtoP) which offers alternative guidance as to when to intervene. RtoP establishes norms of intervention for genocide, humanitarian emergencies, human rights abuses and crimes against humanity but it does not apply to post-natural hazard scenarios.

3.1 Intervention, just intervention and disaster relief

In this section, I explain the notions of intervention, just intervention and disaster relief. I describe these different types of support delivered to those affected by a catastrophe to show the kinds of assistance the international community delivers. In later sections, I argue that if the international community is capable of providing a certain type of assistance in one scenario, then it is unethical to deprive those affected by a different trigger, namely a natural hazard, of the same assistance.

3.1.1 Intervention

First, very generally, an intervention is the interference of one state into the affairs of another.[1] Intervention in its broadest possible meaning, is any unrequested or intrusive meddling into another state's affairs, policies or interaction with a country's people. Economic sanctions, travel restrictions, dismissal of diplomats and so forth are all kinds of interventions; it does not necessarily entail a military component. Traditional intervention theory has its roots in the political philosophy of Saint Augustine and Thomas Aquinas (Fixdal & Smith, 1998). However, what has historically been understood as an intervention has changed as a result of the genocides of the 1990s. Intervention is now typically defined more narrowly and accounts for the use of force.

As it will be used herein, an intervention specifically involves an armed use of force. Holzgrafe begins his definition of this particular type of intervention as follows: "the threat or use of force across state borders by a state (or group of states)" (2003, p. 18). Interventions usually involve foreign powers, organisations or states using force against another state, within which individuals are suffering from some level of crime, violence or deprivation beyond an internationally acceptable threshold (Orend, 2008; Tesón, 2004). This is the definition used for intervention in relation to war and conflict scenarios.

Armed (as opposed to unarmed) intervention faces much scrutiny and as a result it is highly restricted in international law (United Nations, 2015). States are considered to be sovereign, have authority over their own borders and citizens, and thus have a right to non-intervention. At a minimum, any interference without explicit invitation can be considered an act of aggression (United Nations, 2015). At its extreme, interference without invitation can be deemed an act of war. There is still the question as to whether that intervention is just. That is a separate discussion to which I now turn.

3.1.2 Just intervention

There is a distinction to be explained between a just and an unjust intervention. A just intervention is established and carried out within some moral framework. Holzgrefe's definition of intervention considers the human rights of those people for whom the intervention will be carried out. He explains intervention thus:

> the threat or use of force across state borders by a state (or group of states) aimed at preventing or ending widespread and grave violations of the

> fundamental human rights of individuals other than its own citizens, without the permission of the state within whose territory force is applied.
>
> (2003, p. 18)

Here Holzgrefe provides distinct components of an intervention: the use of force, intention to prevent human rights abuses, and a lack of consent.

However, in order for an intervention to be just, the intervening state or international organisation must be able to justify its use of force against another state to the international community on the grounds that it has a duty to intervene (Conces, 2001, p. 138; Fixdal & Smith, 1998, p. 299; Nardin, 2005, p. 22). Importantly, appealing to the need to support human rights is not enough to morally justify an intervention (Conces, 2001, p. 138). Interventions must therefore be justified to the international community using many factors including the sovereignty of an affected state, the financial and political commitment an intervention entails as well as the possible loss of life (see Chapter 6).

Ius ad interventum, or justice in intervening, should be based on foundations similar to those of *ius ad bellum*. Ius ad bellum, or justice in going to war, is the umbrella term used to qualify the actions carried out when a state is deciding to go to war as just. Tesón offers that a (humanitarian) intervention is permissible under the following conditions: it is the

> proportionate international use or threat of military force, undertaken in principle by a liberal government or alliance, aimed at ending tyranny or anarchy, welcomed by the victims, and consistent with the doctrine of double effect.
>
> (2004, p. 94)

These represent the start of the Just War conditions for carrying out a military intervention which will be discussed in Section 3.2.2.

3.1.3 Disaster relief

Interventions for natural hazard response do not occur. Instead of intervening, states usually respond by providing disaster relief. Archibugi explains that aid provided as part of natural hazard response is not intervention at all but rather humanitarian relief. He notes that such relief is delivered with the consent of the affected government in line with norms of disaster relief (Archibugi, 2004).

The Hyogo Framework for Action (HFA), agreed to by most UN member states, sets out the means and goals for the management of disaster response (UNGA, 2014).[2] However, HFA focuses on relief and does not consider whether intervention (when consent for such relief support is not forthcoming) could be required in some natural hazard scenarios. Thus, in order to argue for intervention policy instead of simply disaster relief, I must define disaster relief and explain how it differs from intervention.

"Disaster relief" is the accepted mechanism of response to a disaster: support in response to natural hazards and man-made emergencies which includes the provision of food, shelter and medical supplies (American Red Cross, 2014). The United Nations Office for Disaster Risk Reduction (UNISDR) is charged with coordinating, guiding and monitoring disaster relief and recovery operations globally. The provision of such (natural hazard and other) disaster relief is facilitated by the Emergency Relief Coordinator who first and foremost obtains the consent of the affected parties (UNOCHA, 2014). Thus, while UNISDR coordinates relief at the global level, disaster relief is only delivered once a state government consents to receive it. Then, the operational relief effort is provided in coordination with state governments, NGOs and charities.

While there are policies which dictate the mechanisms of international response to natural hazards, these are inadequate as they rely on consent to or requests for aid. Later I will show that in situations where a government is unable to communicate its needs, policymakers must recognise that there are circumstances in which disaster relief is not enough and intervention should at least be a response option.

3.2 Current grounds for intervention

In order to demonstrate that intervention for the purpose of aiding those affected by natural hazards is appropriate and required, I now explain the current norms of intervention in general terms.[3] I first analyse intervention norms as they already exist. To do this in Section 3.2.1, I discuss why an intervention may be necessary. Objections and problems associated with interventions in general and, more narrowly, in relation to natural hazards will be discussed in Chapter 6. In 3.2.2, I discuss Just War Theory, which sets out the criteria for when "going to war" may be considered just. In 3.2.3, I discuss the Responsibility to Protect doctrine (hereafter RtoP). This doctrine establishes the type of emergency where interventions would be permissible. These two norms are specifically discussed because they each guide decision-making in the use of force in importantly distinct ways and scenarios. I use Just War Theory as a framework for my proposed natural hazard intervention policy in Chapter 7, hence its inclusion and discussion here. RtoP is discussed in this section because it is the established mechanism through which humanitarian interventions are carried out. Accordingly, its positive and negative aspects must be understood in detail so as to understand the likely positive and negative aspects of any newly established intervention policy. RtoP is also discussed in this section to reinforce that current intervention policies do not permit intervention in natural hazard scenarios (as I will explain here and in Section 6.1).

3.2.1 When an intervention may be necessary

When there is an emergency in any sovereign country, the usual first reaction of other countries is to offer assistance and condolences through diplomatic channels. Military forces are usually utilised only when diplomacy has failed. Diplomacy "failing" implies that all non-force types of intervention have been tried and there are no non-military alternatives available to secure peace and security. However, even when diplomacy has failed, force may only be used once further conditions have been met.

Conditions for intervention have been established by the international community; Chapter VII, Article 39 of the UN Charter specifies that an intervention should only occur when there is a "threat to the peace, breach of the peace, or act of aggression". Threats to persons or threats to international peace are specific, officially mandated triggers as to when an intervention can be considered (and thus are possibly just reasons for intervention). These threats can be against persons or international stability more generally.

Protection of those affected. One possible reason for the international community to intervene is to protect those under threat of violence or abuse. However, this reason does not justify intervention in all violent situations. For example, consider an instance where a police officer uses lethal force against a suspected criminal. This is an official act (because it is done by a member of an official state body in an official capacity) carried out against a civilian. Whilst this may be a crime, it is not necessarily a human rights concern for other nations because it does not represent a systematic policy of killing innocent civilians (Pogge, 2008, pp. 63–64). Conversely, officially sanctioned state violence against civilians, or acts of genocide against particular populations, would be likely to qualify as a human rights concern, and arguably justify intervention.

Indeed, the international community usually assumes a duty to intervene when the human rights of a group of people are undermined to such a degree that it "shock(s) the moral conscience of mankind" (Walzer, 1990, p. 107; International Criminal Court, 1998). After World War II, the international community agreed that, when a given people are at risk of harm due to the actions of their own government, the rest of humanity has a duty to intervene to help. The Convention on the Prevention and Punishment of the Crime of Genocide (9 December 1948) was one of the first international conventions setting out grounds and terms of an intervention (ICRC, 2013). Through this and a similar doctrine on humanitarian intervention, the parties to the agreement (currently 147 plus 1 state signatory) assign responsibility to states and individual persons to respond where necessary to aid those facing genocide or a similar threat (ICRC, 2013).

Other triggers for international intervention include: humanitarian emergencies (i.e. a disease outbreak), large-scale human rights abuses (i.e. the forced migration of a population due to government programmes), and war crimes (i.e. the use of biological weapons against civilians). In each case, justification for intervention is grounded in obligations to protect a given population (ICISS, 2001).

Protection of international peace and security. Recent bombings of Islamic State (IS) strongholds have been carried out in response to attacks on Paris in 2015 (Doherty, 2015). IS's intentional killing of a civilian population may be classified as a war crime (International Criminal Court, 2002). This is regardless of the fact that the Paris bombings took place outside a recognised war zone. IS's actions were understood as threats to international peace and security because they undermine international law. The international political system (arguably) has the authority to intervene against IS in this scenario in defence of international peace and security.

Arguments against intervention can be made with reference to Article 2(4) of the UN Charter which explicitly forbids the use of force against the territory or independence of a state. Article 2(7) goes further and explicitly states that nothing in the UN Charter allows for intervention (United Nations, 2015). Diplomacy, trade sanctions, the delivery of humanitarian supplies and so forth are preferred methods of response as any act of force (which would be used in an intervention) is a possible destabilising action. For example, rather than engage in a direct military campaign in the IS example, the United States carried out targeted bombings and attempted to evacuate Yazidis and other Christian groups from Islamic extremist strongholds in 2014 (Spencer, 2014).

In sum, political unrest or mass destruction within a state is not strictly confined to that state and may threaten international (or at least regional) peace and security. Hence, in the current global paradigm, non-intervention as a political norm is not suitable in all situations. To illustrate, Chapter VII of the UN Charter allows for the use of force if there is a threat to international peace and security (United Nations, 2015). It is often invoked when the parties are deciding whether to intervene in the affairs of another country. Thus intervention is required when all possible alternative means of providing assistance have failed and international peace and security are at risk.

3.2.2 Just War Theory

In this and the following section, I outline two dominant paradigms for how and when intervention may be justified: Just War Theory and the Responsibility to Protect. While neither imposes legally binding obligations on states, they are each vitally important to the debate surrounding disaster intervention and shape the context in which interventions are carried out.

Traditional Just War Theory holds that self-defence is the only morally justifiable reason for going to war (Luban, 1980, p. 163). However, modern Just War Theory allows for a broader range of justifications. For example, it has been argued that a just war may be waged "in defense of socially basic human rights" in addition to the traditional view (Luban, 1980, p. 175). While concerns over breaches of sovereignty and territorial integrity do not fall away by using this interpretation of just war, we are at least able to address many of the current global threats carried out by non-state actors, terrorist groups and disasters.

Just War Theory thus provides guiding theoretical principles which can be used in decision-making about going to war or intervening in general. Current Just War Theory sets out individually necessary and jointly sufficient conditions which define when war, or other military intervention short of war, is just. These conditions are:

(a) just cause
(b) right intention
(c) last resort
(d) proportionality
(e) reasonable hope of success
(f) right authority (public declaration)
(g) relative justice (Luban, 1980; Orend, 2008; Walzer, 2006; Fixdal & Smith, 1998).

I discuss each of these conditions in turn below.

(a) *Just cause.* Jeff McMahan explains that a just cause is simply "a good or compelling reason to go to war" (2006, p. 1). Historically, a defender-aggressor relationship exists in which it is possible to determine who has committed a wrong. Furthermore, Johnson explains the Augustinian view that a just cause may be one in which the party intervening or waging war is neither the defender nor the aggressor. Instead, this third party may be defending the innocent from the powerful (1984, p. 22).

Corresponding to this understanding of a just cause, self-defence is explicitly recognised as a legitimate reason for going to war in Article 51 of the UN Charter and thus is entrenched in international law (Fixdal & Smith, 1998, p. 295). When an aggressive act as detailed above is committed against a population, it is just for outside forces to consider commencing an intervention against those committing the aggression. To illustrate this point, consider a recent clash in Eastern Europe in which Russian separatists and Ukrainian forces collided throughout 2014–2015 (Williams, 2015). Even with the death toll rising, a specific group was not targeted and the damage did not hit a level that "shocks the conscience". There may be alternative just causes for intervention into this situation (i.e. stability of the region) but here Ukrainian self-defence in itself can be used as a legitimate reason for going to war.

In more recent literature just cause has been expanded to include prevention of human rights abuses (McMahan, 2006). In these situations, the human rights abuse that qualifies as a just cause will usually include large-scale abuses. The relevant aggressions can include genocide, forced migration of minority groups and other acts involving large numbers of people.

(b) *Right intention.* The second necessary condition for entering a war justly is that the country that does so acts with a right intention. A right intention aims at preserving human dignity and/or at creating international peace and security. It should not be driven solely by selfish motives. Accordingly, an intervening state must make the case to the international community that it has a right intention and thus the "motive for responding to the cause and taking up the goals" must be just (Fixdal & Smith, 1998, p. 286).

The major reason declared by the United States in their decision to attack Iraq in 2003 was Iraq's possession of weapons of mass destruction (Record, 2003). The stated fear was that the threat posed by these weapons in the hands of "rogue states" could not be met with a policy of deterrence alone (Record, 2003, p. 3). The possibility that such weapons could be used against neighbouring countries meant that they were a threat to international peace and security. While inspection of the sites never found evidence of WMDs, the stated intention with this intervention was to respond to imminent aggression thereby meeting the "just war" condition.

There are, of course, those who argue that a "new imperialism" was actually the driver behind the US invasion of Iraq. Terry Nardin explains that the United States replaced the rhetoric of "barbaric practices" once used to justify imperialism with "tyranny and terrorism" as justifications for intervention in the name of humanity (2005, p. 25). The true "intention" is therefore unclear and so determining whether this intervention had a right intention, and hence was just, remains open.

(c) *Last resort.* There will likely be situations in which a just cause exists and interveners' intentions are motivated by humanitarian concerns. In these situations, the last resort condition requires that all actions short of military engagement have already been exhausted before force can be used. Diplomacy, trade sanctions and other actions that do not use force should be attempted before military action is taken.

Some groups or politicians might argue that there are alternatives to going to war that have not been considered or tried. The last resort condition for just war can hence be quite difficult to prove. However, all attempts at resolving the situation without using force should be carried out before the use of force is entertained as a response option. Thus, according to the standards of Just War Theory, going to war can be just only when all other options have been exhausted and the use of force is the very last resort.

(d) *Proportionality.* When going to war, the intervener must prove that the use of force is a proportional response to the aggression being committed. Conces explains that this principle is simply "a matter of weighing the consequences of the various military options that are available" (2001, p. 147). For example, using nuclear weapons against a state that is using outdated, conventional military equipment to defend itself is not a proportionate response. Proportionality, instead, is about using the right amount of force so that aggressions are halted. McMahan explains that proportionality is a separate criteria from just cause in that it is wholly about the "scale, magnitude or comparable importance" of going to war (2006, p. 4). In this way, proportionality is the measurable aspect of Just War Theory.

Similarly, the cost to an intervener's own military and its domestic population contribute to the proportionality condition of just war. A long and costly invasion period may undermine the economic or physical security of the people in the intervening country. Proportionality requires that the citizens of the intervening country are not unduly burdened by the intervention such that it undermines their lives and livelihoods. If it does undermine their lives and livelihoods the duties associated with the political and economic rights of the people in the intervening country are not being addressed.

Consider the invasion of Afghanistan after the 2001 terrorist attacks as an example. Let us apply the proportionality condition alone to this scenario and put to one side the just cause or right intention conditions. It can be argued that the US-led coalition invasion of Afghanistan in 2003 was not a proportionate response because of the costs to life and livelihood incurred by US and Afghani citizens. The United States also had an enormous advantage in terms of military capability. Using this hardware to invade a country which only had access to antiquated guns and tanks is likely disproportionate.

(e) *Reasonable hope of success.* The Afghanistan example forces us to question whether there was ever a reasonable hope of success for this intervention. When considering the use of force, there must be a reasonable hope that the use of force will actually improve the welfare situation for those affected and for international peace and security. A clear operational and strategic plan must be developed before the intervention is put into action. An exit plan is also necessary. If a country becomes dependent on the invading force, the invasion has failed in its attempt to re-stabilise a state and thus to re-establish international peace and security.

If there is no reasonable hope of success, the invading force is putting the affected population at further risk of death whilst meanwhile putting its own forces at risk. One way to measure the success of a military operation is to determine the number of lives lost (or at a minimum negatively affected). An intervention which haphazardly puts its military at risk did not have a reasonable hope of success in the first place. By fulfilling just war criteria we limit the injustice acted upon those already affected by the emergency. If the population affected or the population responding are expected to be made worse off by the war, then it has not filled this necessary condition of having a reasonable hope of success.

(f) *Right authority.* The intervening force must have a right authority for an intervention to be just. Those with legitimate authority to declare war include states and international bodies. Individuals or groups of any sort do not have such authority to wage war and instead their use of force is usually considered rebellion or terrorism. The right authority condition can also be understood as a requirement for an international approval for an intervention. When all of the other just war criteria are met, the international community may authorise the use of force.

(g) *Relative justice.* There are, thus, very clear conditions under which the use of force is claimed to be "just". Collectively, these conditions form the theoretical framework for waging a just war. Even though this list is detailed and wide-ranging, it is not exhaustive. Each conflict requires independent consideration with the scenario reviewed in isolation. Other, similar interventions should be studied, but the grounds for intervention are not and should not be dependent on whether war was waged in a "similar" situation previously. The just war conditions should be considered on their own merit each time there is an impetus for going to war.

In this section I have outlined the conditions for waging a just war. These same criteria are not considered when deciding whether to intervene after a natural hazard as they are removed from this (and most) analyses of the just use of force. In Chapter 6, I explain that Just War Theory should be applied when developing intervention policy post-natural hazard.

3.2.3 *Responsibility to Protect*

The Responsibility to Protect doctrine is another way of determining when a military intervention is just. While modern Just War Theory is the outcome of ongoing historical debates, the Responsibility to Protect is a very recent theoretical and practical development. The Responsibility to Protect has emerged as a doctrine central to humanitarian intervention debates and is therefore highly important for the purposes of my analysis as to whether intervention as a part of natural hazard response could ever be morally appropriate and required. I will provide an overview explanation of the origin and use of the Responsibility to Protect including (a) a background of its development, (b) its processes, priorities and the way in which it is delivered, and finally (c) how it is used in international affairs. I will end this section by discussing why RtoP has not been, nor should be, applied to natural hazard situations.

(a) *Background.* In the aftermath of the Rwandan genocide, Kofi Annan (then Secretary General of the United Nations) challenged the international community to avoid situations where it was "united but ineffective" in responding to the life and death needs of foreign populations when faced with such things as deprivation of food and water and violence against the person (Wheeler, 2005, p. 3). The International Commission on Intervention and State Sovereignty (ICISS) was established by the Canadian Government as a response to Annan's suggestion that consensus on a global "humanitarian intervention" doctrine was necessary: RtoP was the output of this commission (ICISS, 2001).

The aim of RtoP was to establish effective guidelines for future military interventions. It specifies that the international community has a responsibility to intervene into a sovereign state if there is a collective decision that individuals are at risk due to genocide, human rights abuses, humanitarian emergency or war crimes (ICISS, 2001). When originally discussed, natural hazards were considered for inclusion. However, they were left out of the final doctrine (and the resulting norm) because it was not possible to garner sufficient political support for their inclusion. International consensus and the eventual adoption of RtoP were only possible because it restricted the type of emergencies in which RtoP would be triggered (Cohen, 2008). Consequently, natural hazards were purposefully left out.

It has even been argued that invoking RtoP to justify interventions in natural hazard situations is inappropriate (Evans, 2008; Thakur, 2008; International Coalition for the Responsibility to Protect, 2008). Casualties of earthquakes, tsunamis, volcanoes, etc. were considered simply "death caused by natural disasters" and did not require any additional support (Thakur, 2008). Furthermore, it is claimed that a natural hazard intervention would make an intervention for genocide and crimes against humanity more difficult as it would increase the frequency of interventions thus depleting international resources and political will (Evans, 2008).

(b) *Process, priorities and delivery.* RtoP justifies the use of force at the different stages of implementation (ICISS, 2001, pp. 69–70). As for process, the ICISS stressed that any intervention must reflect a collective responsibility to protect, meaning that the international community must come together and agree to take action. Each party then bears a portion of the responsibility for intervening and for the consequences of the intervention. (This hints at both the acceptance of the universality of human rights and the idea that a right authority must authorise this type of intervention.) Focus on collective responsibility is intended to avoid actual or perceived unilateral action and the potential that it is used merely to further the ends of the intervening agent. To illustrate, it may be argued that unilateral airstrikes organised by one nation would be likely to only represent that nation's interests. There would be limited debate and assessment of whether intervening in a given scenario would be a just intervention and therefore would not represent a collective responsibility.

RtoP is intended to provide the official means necessary to enable the international community to react to large-scale human rights abuses. In addition to being reactive, society must also have plans which prevent the occurrence of atrocities. Hence, the Responsibility to Protect was established alongside the responsibility to prevent and to rebuild (UN General Assembly, 2009, p. 2). In particular circumstances prevention will no longer be possible. At that point, and when all other options of engagement with the unfriendly state have been exhausted, delivery of assistance through armed intervention may be deemed appropriate. RtoP thereby sets out the standards against which reacting to large-scale human rights abuses by way of an intervention is judged.

(c) *RtoP in practice.* The RtoP is a moral responsibility of states and not a legally binding international mandate. While not explicit in Chapter VII of the UN Charter, the RtoP is often argued for (and thus endorsed by the international community) through the invocation of the UN Charter. At the same time, implementation of Chapter VII of the UN Charter requires vast international consensus and hence is rarely utilised. Additionally, the 2005 World Summit Outcome document, accepted by the UN General Assembly, formally established this norm of international response for the international community (UN General Assembly, 2005).

Both Chapter VII of the UN Declaration and the RtoP doctrine highlight the need for coordination when intervening. By intervening under the auspices of RtoP, interveners are assuring the international community's operations will be carried out in coordination, or at least in consultation, with global policy makers. This helps to justify that the intervention has a right intention – it is not being done under false or self-serving pretences. Additionally, the interveners are stating that the intervention is being carried out to protect and not to dominate a foreign population. Furthermore, invoking RtoP requires precise justifications that the situation has escalated to such a point that military intervention is the only option left. Hence, RtoP creates a policy and supports intervention in line with just war conditions.

RtoP doctrine is thus an accepted foundation for intervention. However, by promoting military intervention, RtoP normatively conflicts with the assumption of non-intervention enshrined in the UN Declaration and made possible by the existence of the sovereign state system. This dichotomy suggests that non-intervention and intervention can exist in international norms simultaneously. Accordingly, there is precedent for military intervention to protect humans as long as certain criteria of justice are met. RtoP is only used as a last resort. It can therefore be argued that Article 41 leaves space for engaging with RtoP in situations where all other non-military options for engagement have been exhausted.

I have here discussed RtoP in order to show that interventions to save humans in a crisis have been debated at high levels of international governance and RtoP has been found to be a necessary policy. I am not including discussion of RtoP here in order to argue that natural hazards should be included in the list of emergencies which trigger RtoP. Indeed, the exclusion of natural hazards as a trigger for intervention in RtoP ensures that peacekeeping operations for genocide, humanitarian emergencies, human rights abuses and war crimes will continue to receive at least some support by the international community. However, natural hazards do need their own policy which establishes criteria for a just intervention. In my argument of Chapter 6, RtoP will serve as a background and provide support for the idea that intervention for natural hazard response is justifiable.

3.3 Conclusion

In this chapter, I have provided analysis of intervention policy as it currently exists. I have defined intervention and made the distinction between just and unjust interventions. I then explained that disaster relief is currently the only means of response to natural hazards and does not involve intervention, whilst military forces are sometimes used to deliver assistance. I also explained general issues which any intervention will have to take into account.

In the final section of this chapter, I explained the two traditional frameworks for understanding when interventions are just – Just War Theory and the Responsibility to Protect. These normative frameworks provide a base from which intervention policy for natural hazard scenarios can be built in the following chapters. My goal in doing so was to provide an outline of the existing intervention policies available to responders, to show that natural hazards are purposely not included, and provide an overview of the precedent set by these other norms of intervention. In the next chapter I make my argument for why intervention policy for natural hazards is appropriate and necessary.

Notes

1 For a discussion on the varying degrees of intervention, see (Holzgrefe, 2003, p. 18; Tesón, 2004).
2 The post-2015 framework for disaster risk reduction is intended to compliment the Hyogo Framework for Action (2005–2015) and asserts the "plan of action" (UNGA, 2014, pp. 3–4).
3 For the sake of brevity any suggestion of an intervention should be assumed to be a just intervention unless otherwise stated.

4 Welfare as a human right

The central ethical concept of this chapter will be that of rights. There are three central components to any right: the right-holder, the addressee and the scope of the right (Nickel, 2013). I am only concerned, however, with one family of human rights: welfare rights (Nickel, 2013, p. 181). The scope of this family of rights, as I will argue, is a minimal level of food, shelter, water, security and health care. This should be provided by the state as the addressee of the right. I will argue in later chapters that a natural hazard and the disruption it causes to a society may prevent the delivery of the goods included in what constitutes a basic level of welfare. However, the right to a basic minimum of welfare during a disaster is a human right and thus must be guaranteed by the addressees of the relevant human rights no matter the circumstances. Therefore, as I argue below, if a government is unable or unwilling to act as the addressee of the right to welfare, some other duty holder must step in.

In 4.1, I first subject the concept of human rights to a conceptual analysis including an explanation of how human rights differ from other rights. In 4.2, I focus on the human right to welfare and the scope of this right. In Section 4.3, I explore the main ways in which the human right to welfare can be grounded: in the badness of pain and suffering, our interdependence and our joint humanity. I argue that the grounding based on a joint humanity is most appropriate because it consistently includes all right-holders without exception. In Section 4.4, I address possible criticisms of using human rights as the justification for developing international policy as I suggest.

4.1 Human rights in general

For context, there are various types of rights – political, civil, economic – and there are commonalities amongst these categories of rights: all rights have claimants, duty-bearers and a scope of the right. Take the political right to protest, for example. A member of the Occupy Movement, as a right-holder, had a political right to protest outside St Paul's Cathedral and Parliament in London. The British Government, despite their frustration, were the addressee and thus had the duty to ensure that the Occupy member's right to protest was upheld. The scope of this right is free speech in protest of what the movement saw as institutionalised economic and social wrongs.

Furthermore, rights can be understood either as moral or legal rights. Many civil, political and social rights are enshrined in national laws so that they can be enforced at the national level. Some of these rights are also accounted for in international doctrine and agreements for additional assurance of legal implementation such as the right to be free from torture, the right to take part in elections and so forth. As a consequence, the addressees of these legal rights have legal obligations as set out by laws of a particular jurisdiction. For my purposes, I concentrate on moral rights which include universal rights such as the right to liberty or autonomy. What distinguishes moral rights from legal rights is that the addressees of these rights have, instead of legal obligations, moral obligations corresponding to the relevant right. I am interested in moral rights because whilst laws and hence legal rights can change, the moral facet of rights remains constant and universal across jurisdiction.

Hence I am only concerned with human rights as a particular kind of moral rights, not their legal basis. In this section, I first explain the three features which make human rights distinct from other rights and which are central to understanding and applying human rights to this topic. Human rights are universal, set minimum standards and are "high priority" norms (Nickel, 2013; Caney, 2010). Next I explain why I reject the other features of human rights (Nickel sets out a list of eight features) as distinguishing them from other rights (Nickel, 2013).

First, unlike other rights, human rights are universal. Human rights extend to *every human person* regardless of gender, race, or religion, at all times. Likewise, national political borders do not matter as to whether or not a country's inhabitants have human rights. Each human has a claim to the scope of the right in question. For example, I am a resident in the United Kingdom. As an American citizen, I do not have all political rights available to citizens of this country (voting, for example). However, my human rights are exactly the same as British citizens. Accordingly, I have a claim to the scope of a given human right, say welfare, no matter the country I am living in or whether I have political rights as a woman. Human rights are in this sense universal.[1]

Second, unlike many other rights, human rights can also be understood to set a minimum global standard to which each rights-holder is entitled. Human rights do not guarantee me the "right" to a lavish lifestyle or the "right" to a home well above my economic means. From a moral perspective, human rights establish the foundation upon which all other types of rights can be built. If they guaranteed more than minimum standards they would be too prescriptive to be agreed upon widely. I can have a decent life without gas heating (specifically, for example) as long as I am safe and healthy within my home. (Other sources of warmth may be sufficient.) Whilst gas heating may be preferable in some societies it is not a basic, necessary good of the type which human rights are often thought to protect.[2]

Instead, many have argued that human rights underpin efforts to support humans developing minimally decent lives (Nussbaum, 2007a). We each have the right not to be killed and to be given fair treatment under the law with regard to our gender, race or religion. By setting minimum standards human rights set a standard for humans to be treated with a basic level of dignity and humanity (see Section 5.3).

As a consequence, the addressees of human rights are duty-bound to ensure that a minimum threshold of necessary goods is available for a person to exercise their human rights. This means that duty-bearers, for example, are not allowed to provide humans in their charge any less than a standard minimum. In fact, governments are encouraged to offer citizens more in the way of civic rights and many do through political and economic policies. Human rights, though, are assurances that humans will have a minimally decent life in line with what is physically and compassionately necessary for any human (Pogge, 2008, p. 55).

Third, human rights are the highest moral concern for society or, as Nickel describes them, "high priority norms" (2013; Cranston, 1967). National governments have an interest in providing certain rights to their citizens – a well-functioning economy, for example, will mean stability and higher quality of life for citizens. However, human rights, claimed by all humans, are the "highest priority" – they "trump" or, rather, generally prevail over, all other claims (Nickel, 1987). Consider that a national government may want to pursue a development agenda for the good of its people. In pursuing that, the national government cannot fail in its responsibility to ensure that individuals have fair and equal access to the goods associated with that development and/or that in pursuing that development goal, some individuals will have to go without nutritious food (Shue, 1980; Nickel, 1987, pp. 16–17, 2013, 2017).[3]

I argue for universality, minimal standards and high priority norms as the main features of human rights because they are applicable across all human rights and thus appropriately make sense of rights. The other features of rights as set out by Nickel – namely that human rights are not dependent on the procedures of a national government, that they provide global standards against which national governments can be judged, that they are specific and that they establish political norms – are important but not relevant within the context of this analysis.

For example, if we say human rights are "specific" we are limiting the situations and cases in which they can be applied. Consider that human rights imply that all humans are entitled to dignity. There is general agreement as to how we treat a human with dignity (torture is bad, disrespecting a corpse is bad, etc.). However, if we specified the exact parameters of a dignified life we would not be able to make allowances for autonomous choices made over the course of one's life. If we specified what dignity must entail we would either not account for everyone's dignified life and/or not be able to treat everyone with dignity. Disposing of remains, for instance, varies by country and culture and each is seen as dignified within that culture. Requiring that we set the parameters of a dignified treatment after death would be too specific. With this kind of justification in mind, I have chosen the three features of human rights which I argue help us distinguish human rights as a unique type of right.

4.2 A Human right to welfare

I am interested in the family of welfare rights and the recognition of associated duties in natural hazard response. So, in this section I first explain welfare more broadly. Second, I show how the human right to welfare matches the features of human rights discussed in the previous section.

4.2.1 An explanation of welfare

We can start from the idea that welfare, or well-being, is an evaluation of how good (or well) a person's state of being is as opposed to the "good" that they provide (Sen, 1993, p. 36). If a person's life goes well and she is in a good state, she has a high level of welfare independently of how useful she is for the society. Welfare as it is used in the human rights literature is thus an internal state of being. It is not to be confused with "welfare" in the way of housing or social benefits.

There are different ways of understanding welfare which could all be argued to help measure how good one's life is going by one's own standards. Traditionally there are three theories of well-being: hedonism, desire-satisfaction and objective-list theories. In what follows I explain each. For hedonism and desire-satisfaction I explain why these are inadequate ways of making sense of welfare, particularly as it pertains to emergency situations.

Hedonism, at its most basic, is understood as the balance of pleasure over pain in one's life (Crisp, 2016). If one's life contains a lot of pleasures and very few pains, then, according to hedonism, one's life is going well and one has a high level of welfare. In contrast, if one's life contains mainly painful experiences and suffering, then on this view one has a low level of welfare.

There is one main objection to pleasure as the core of well-being in the natural hazard context that I raise here. Consider hedonistic welfare in terms of disaster response; responders provide life-saving and life-sustaining aid to those they are rescuing. If hedonism were the correct account of welfare relevant for the human right to welfare, then instead of providing people with food, drink and shelter, the responders could simply hand out pleasure pills, since this would also provide the victims with the same increase in their welfare. However, the removal of suffering, particularly in this situation, only results in a different state of mind whereas the person's physical condition is still unchanged – they may still be homeless, hungry or remain stuck under rubble (Sen, 1985, pp. 188–189). This must be an implausible consequence of the theory. Surely the right thing to say is that, if the responders care about the victim's welfare, they ought to save the victims' lives by providing them with food, drink, shelter and other constituents of their welfare. This is why it is not plausible to think that the relevant notion of welfare here consists of mere pleasure.

The second theory of well-being is desire-satisfaction. According to desire-satisfaction theory, something improves overall well-being if it satisfies one's desires (Hooker, 2000, p. 39). On this view, the more a person's desires, plans, intentions and so on are satisfied, the higher that person's level of welfare is, and vice versa. More specifically, many defenders of this view argue that it is the satisfaction of intrinsic desires that make our lives go well (Heathwood, 2006). Intrinsic desires are desires for those things that we desire for their own sake. So, we do not desire money for its own sake; we only desire it because it enables us to get those things we desire. Hence desire-satisfaction can be said to come from obtaining those things which satisfy intrinsic desires.

However, a desire-satisfaction theory of well-being fails because not all the things we desire intrinsically can be good or right for us (Fletcher, 2013; Hooker, 2000, p. 39). For example, I may desire to have 50 children. I have an intrinsic desire to be a mother and give birth multiple times and to share my life with as many children as possible. As Griffin explains, we cannot exclude immoral or irrational desires from those that should be satisfied in order for a person to achieve well-being if those are the person's actual desires (1988/2003, p. 24). Accordingly, this irrational desire would need to be satisfied in order for me to have a high level of welfare on this view.

A second problem with desire-satisfaction as a foundation of welfare comes from the literature on adaptive preferences (Nussbaum, 1997; Moss, 2013). According to Amartya Sen, desires (as mental characteristics) adjust to circumstances: our expectations for which and how our desires can be satisfied are diminished by what is possible in a given life scenario (Sen, 1999). Consider adaptive preferences in the following example: Person A is financially poor, lives in a functional but basic house, and can just about feed her family. She feels that she has everything she desires in life. In contrast, Person B is financially wealthy: she can afford a mortgage on a lavish house and goes on foreign vacations every year. She desires a new car, HD TV and the newest iPhone. Person B feels the absence of the goods she desires and yet does not have. She would thus have a low level of well-being according to the desire-satisfaction theory because her desires have not been satisfied. If we care about other people's welfare, desire-satisfaction theory would in this situation require that we provide for the desires of Person B. Given that she has a lower level of well-being, we have a requirement to provide for her needs over Person A's. This would, in essence, penalise Person A for having adapted her preference for things which she could not obtain (Van Parijs, 2004). However, no one would believe that Person B is leading a poor life (except maybe Person B). Adaptive preferences as an objection to desire-satisfaction theory helps to demonstrate that desire-satisfaction theory will not be objective in to whom and how rights are distributed and restricts our ability to make "interpersonal comparisons of well-being and deprivation" (Sen, 1999, pp. 62–63). Hence, desire-satisfaction theory does not account for the inequality of each individual as a starting point.

The third theory of well-being is that of an objective list. On this view, a person has a high level of welfare when she has a sufficient amount of certain objective goods (Rice, 2013). Furthermore, it doesn't matter whether the person enjoys having those goods or wants to have them in her life. Those basic goods represent things that would make each individual person's life better. Hence these basic goods are universal and would be the same across cultures and therefore can be said to be an "objective" or neutral way of determining welfare.[4] Different goods are included on "objective lists" depending on which list is used: loving relationships, knowledge, autonomy, friendship and achievement are, for example, often included on the list (Rice, 2013; Hooker, 2000).[5]

How should we determine which items should be on the list? Many people have thought that the capabilities approach is the most plausible answer to this question. The "capabilities approach", as an objective-list view, has often been used as a guiding principle when drafting international development policy. Items on this objective list include: life; bodily health; bodily integrity; senses, imagination and thought; emotions; practical reason; affiliation; other species; play; control over one's environment (Nussbaum, 2001, 2011). The listed items within the capabilities approach are determined to be those things necessary for a person to carry out normal functioning, that is, for doing the kind of things that are typical activities for human beings generally.

Considering the human right to welfare, we should focus on the most basic items to be guaranteed in an emergency situation. These goods also belong to any plausible account of what the most basic welfare of human beings consists of; it is difficult to see how one could live a decent human life without them. Presumably they belong to all objective lists concerning human welfare. I am not suggesting that these items guarantee the flourishing life of an individual. Instead, these are the objectively necessary goods for one to be able to survive and are necessary for health. After these items have been obtained, a person can build on their capabilities.

There is one major criticism against object-list theories of rights (such as the capabilities approach). Critics sometimes suggest that an objective-list theory is paternalistic (or elitist) in that it sets out what is good for someone (Crisp, 2016). This criticism aligns with the suggestion that human rights, and intervention in support of human rights, are western inventions imposed on other countries (see Lauta, 2016). I will address this related criticism in detail in Section 6.3.1. For now it is sufficient to explain that autonomy is usually included in an objective list of goods which enable the right bearer to obtain welfare (Hooker, 2000). Autonomous choice about how one lives one's life will at least be a balance against paternalistic intentions of those providing the goods associated with the right.

And so, the objective-list theory of well-being allows for universal application and the setting of minimum standards of a specific set of goods/services. I will assume the objective-list approach to welfare when discussing the human right to welfare.

4.2.2 The human right to welfare

In this section, I introduce how a human right to welfare as argued for would need to be universal, provide a minimum standard, and be a high priority. Then, in the rest of this chapter, I will argue that there is such a right.

First, a human right to welfare would need to have the relevant component parts: the right-holder, an addressee and a scope. As a human right, every human being would be a right-holder. We all would have a legitimate claim to everything that falls under the scope of the right. As a consequence, the state would need to enforce and ensure our right to basic welfare (basic levels of food, water, shelter and medical care). These goods are needed by all humans to survive. These are universally necessary goods and are not contingent on what a national government policy dictates. Even if my church group tries to support me with food from a food bank, ultimately, my government must ensure the right. In this way, the state would be the primary duty-bearer.[6]

I move now to discussing the components of the human right to welfare which would make it distinctly a human right. First, the human right to welfare would be a right to a *basic minimum* of welfare. As explained, and for the purpose of disaster response, it is only necessary to argue for a *basic minimum* of welfare rights which includes food, shelter, essential medical attention and basic levels of security (Shue, 1980, p. 19; Griffin, 2008, p. 90).[7] Some may question how much of these basic goods are necessary for fulfilment of the right; I will not attempt to suggest actual amounts. Instead, the goods associated with the human right to welfare must be provided such that the basic needs of the people in question are met (and they survive in the aftermath of the emergency).

The goods associated with the human right to welfare as described herein allow for the realisation of other rights. The human right to basic welfare need not include education, comprehensive health care and long-term support as I qualify it herein. An education or social interaction which would enable a person to achieve things in life cannot be enjoyed if individuals are suffering and cannot take advantage of those rights (Shue, 1980, pp. 19–20). Thus, in line with Henry Shue's view, the human right to welfare, if there were such a right, would be of the *highest priority* because other rights, say to education, are only possibly claimed if one continues to be alive. Food, on the other hand, is required. Accordingly, food, shelter, medical attention and security are of the highest moral concern for society (Nickel, 2013).

As the highest moral concern, the international community has moral justification for putting pressure on a state to fulfil its duties.[8] For example, the international community has a moral justification for pressurizing the North Korean regime for their non-adherence to human rights norms because human right to basic food, water, shelter is of more importance than government systems. Once the people are secure, pressure can be brought to bear regarding other aspects of the government's dictatorial regime. The welfare of North Koreans is indeed a high priority and must be secured before any other political or economic rights are possible.

Finally, the human right to welfare understood as a guarantee of a minimum level of goods necessary for survival could be argued to be a universal standard. The amount of food, water, etc. that a person requires to continue living does not change based on a person's nationality, race, sexual orientation, etc. In this way a basic minimum applies to all humans, everywhere, equally.

To summarise, the central features of human rights would also characterise the human right to welfare if there is such a right. The human right to welfare must be universally applicable to all humans, it must set a minimum standard and it must be a high priority norm. In the next section, I outline three ways in which the human right to welfare can be justified. This lays the groundwork for my argument made in later chapters that interventions are in some cases ethically required because of the human right to welfare.

4.3 Grounding the human right to welfare

I now discuss different ways to ground the human right to welfare. This is important for my argument made later that the duties associated with the human right to welfare must be acted upon in post-natural hazard emergency situations. Three kinds of justifications for this right were offered in the previous section. These arguments can be based on (i) the moral significance of suffering, (ii) the role of human interaction, and (iii) the importance of respecting humanity. I argue that the first two justifications for the human right to welfare fail but the third does not. Towards the end of this section and especially in subsequent chapters, I consider some specific consequences the resulting understanding of the human right to welfare has for how the international community should react to emergencies triggered by natural hazards.

4.3.1 The badness of pain and suffering

First, the universal human right to welfare could be argued to exist for the simple reason that pain and suffering are bad. All members of a moral community (including all humans, all "marginal cases", and all non-human animals) can suffer and feel pain and because of this it could be claimed that they all deserve equal moral consideration (Shafer-Landau, 2012, p. 131; Singer, 1972).[9] To illustrate, if someone is trapped in a burning building, all reasonable efforts should be made to save her. Likewise, the family pet ought to be carried out of that building because it is generally accepted that burning causes pain even for animals and pain is bad.

Singer argues more specifically that all of us are morally required to prevent pain and suffering if it is something we are able to do and the prevention will not cause greater suffering to ourselves or others (1972, p. 232). This would mean that every suffering person is entitled to (and thus can make a claim for) help and we are all required (have a duty) to help suffering persons. In Singer's famous example, if a child is drowning as you pass a pond, you are morally required to assist that child, even if it means getting your clothes dirty (Singer, 1972). This is because getting muddy is nowhere near as bad as a child's death. By saving the child we are maximizing welfare. If we extend this example to a natural hazard emergency, saving the life of a drowning victim, when responders are qualified to do so and hence will not be hurt themselves, is obviously expected. This too will reduce the pain of the individual affected and by extension the welfare of the community.[10] If a person is faced with two options, they should pick the option that will ultimately bring about the most pleasure. If pain and suffering are bad it is reasonable to expect people to minimise suffering where possible. Grounding human rights in the badness of pain and suffering view is, however, unsuitable, as I will now explain.

If we try to ground the human right to welfare on badness of pain, then it follows that there should be as little pain and suffering as possible. Hence this grounding of the human right seems to lead to utilitarian welfare maximisation. A problem with grounding the human right to welfare in this way is that we would have to let certain people suffer in order to minimise suffering overall. Consider the recent protests against the Dakota Access Pipeline across the northern border of the United States (Aisch & Lai, 2017). The US government's argument for a pipeline in the area is that millions of Americans will benefit from the oil transported through it. Any risks associated with oil transportation are acceptable because of the benefit the oil will provide. This is in spite of the pain and suffering caused to members of the Sioux living on the Standing Rock Reservation.

However, this does not fit with human rights theory. Human rights are universal and must therefore protect everyone's welfare equally. Likewise, because human rights are universal we cannot sacrifice one person's well-being for the sake of others. Thus the alleviation of pain and suffering grounding does not provide the individual with protection; it puts overall society's well-being above the individual. Human rights dictate that the individual human is the claimant of any human right and thus any duties must provide the goods associated with the right to the individual.

So, whilst the badness of pain and suffering is a reason to supply goods associated with the human right to welfare, it is not the most appropriate grounding for the human right to welfare. This grounding does not help to ensure that goods will be distributed equally and universally to all humans as required by the universality of human rights. Therefore, it can be rejected as an appropriate grounding of the human right to welfare.

4.3.2 Interaction-based human right to welfare

The second way to ground the human right to welfare is to argue that it is justified by the connections that exist between persons. In this section, I begin with a description of a frontier community and explain how "special" relationships exist in such communities. From here I argue that there is no moral reason to assume special relationships stop at national borders. Hence "relevant interactions" need not stop at national borders either and likewise, the associated duties do not stop at borders. However, I then argue that by taking "relevant interactions" at its core, the interdependence-based grounding is an inappropriate way to ground the human right to welfare.

To begin, frontier communities are a simple example of people who depend on each other for survival and have a "mutual concern" for one another. With "mutual concern" it can be argued that "everyone benefits from being in the community – mutual protection, some division of labour, social life, and so on" (Griffin, 2008, p. 178). Each inhabitant relies on the other inhabitants for their survival: a blacksmith is equally important to a farmer or a cattle rancher. Each person plays a part and as a consequence of their contribution they have a right to assistance from the community to which they have contributed. This simple example can thus be used to illustrate the idea that certain kinds of interaction within communities can be argued to create rights to assistance for the members of those communities.

It can then be argued, similarly, that that same kind of right-creating cooperation and reciprocity exists between citizens within national boundaries in a state. Such cooperation can thus be argued to create a "special" national relationship as a consequence of which, within a sovereign state, citizens have various political rights and also rights to assistance. Based on the interaction between them, citizens certain things and we can say that they have rights within their country.

However, even if we accept that intra-state relationships are special, there is no moral reason to assume that we do not *also* have the relevant kind of special relationships of interaction with those outside the political borders within which we live. For example, I have strong familial ties to the United States. However, I have studied abroad and now have relationships with people living in a different country. I would be as worried about their safety in an earthquake as I would be about members of my family. Special bonds with my family and co-nationals do not prohibit me from having the relevant relationships with friends outside my country of origin. But, these relationships do suggest that we can be interconnected with those outside our national boundaries in a way that similarly creates duties and rights for all of us.

It follows, then, that if we think that reciprocal interaction within a state creates a moral entitlement for assistance from other people within the state, then it is appropriate to think that universal interaction provides the same kind of entitlements universally. This would mean that interaction would, in fact, create a universal human right to welfare. In this tradition, we have duties of justice to all of those with whom we interact (Moellendorf, 2002, p. 31).

In a discussion of human rights grounded in interdependence, it is worth discussing the support provided by cosmopolitan theory. Institutional cosmopolitanism is based on this interdependence-based view of human rights (Pogge, 2011; Caney, 2010). These cosmopolitans claim that there are "duties of justice to some, but not all persons," as long as that duty is delivered to *all* "of the persons with whom we are associated" (Moellendorf, 2002, p. 34).[11] This is not to say that certain people do not have a right to welfare. Moellendorf does not suggest that certain humans have rights to welfare and others do not. He only suggests that an individual or official's duty of justice does not extend further than to those with whom we have some sort of associational relationship. Indeed, persons only have moral duties to one another if they are relationally or institutionally linked (Moellendorf, 2002, pp. 32–33). By extension, if we interact with an individual in a relevant way we are morally required to deliver the goods associated with the human right to welfare. Accordingly, grounding the human right to welfare in interdependence excludes, in theory, those with whom we do not share a connection from receiving basic welfare goods. I have three criticisms of this grounding of human rights: (1) the issue of isolated communities, (2) the possibility that we will make badly off people worse off, and (3) a practical problem of deciding who to help. I will discuss these objections in turn.

First, if the interdependence-based grounding of the human right to welfare were the correct grounding of the human right in question, we would not be morally obligated to assist isolated communities. Consider the following: In 2014, Ireland held the Presidency of the European Council. At that time, North Korea was cut off from all trade with western countries and it was not a member of the United Nations. It is therefore fair to assume that Ireland and North Korea did not have a trade relationship. Let us assume further that very few if any North Koreans lived in Ireland and thus cultural links with North Korea were minimal or possibly non-existent. It could be argued that from the interdependence-based view of the human right to welfare, Ireland did not have a duty to provide assistance to North Korea in the event of a tsunami or earthquake because there were no official links or relationships between the two countries.

Hence, if we were strict adherents to the interdependence-based grounding of the human right to welfare, there would be no duty to ensure the human right to welfare to those we do not interact with in a "relevant way". However, this is not how the world works in reality. Indeed, during such an emergency response welfare is not delivered to those with whom a group has a relationship only: no group of people is officially excluded from the international community, no matter their status as pariah state or otherwise.[12] Intuitively the international community sees it as a duty to provide assistance to other humans (even if they do not always act on that duty). This can be seen in situations where the international community air drops supplies for people affected by emergencies when in isolated areas or countries. We may consider whether dropping supplies is politically appropriate, is helpful to the overall situation, and will not exacerbate an existing conflict before delivering aid. What we do not consider is whether our relationship with those suffering is "a relevant type of relationship". In this way, interdependence does not in fact ground the human right to welfare. If it did people within pariah states would not receive air drops of assistance when required.

Second, by grounding the right to welfare in interdependence we are arguably perpetuating systems which disadvantage those that are already badly off. Our global economic and political systems already disadvantage poor and/or developing countries. Thomas Pogge has forcefully argued that the global poor are disadvantaged because of the way in which the rich countries have divided up resources to their own advantage (2001). In this regard, the global poor can be said to have been purposefully harmed by interactions. This perpetuates unequal political and economic systems and is not consistent with the universality of human rights. Instead, consider an individual already excluded from international economic and political systems, such as a farmer in rural Africa.

Caney has explained that some interdependent notions of cosmopolitanism assume that we *may* have duties of humanitarian assistance to those outside traditional systems of economics and politics (2009). This "may", however, is still problematic in that it does not *ensure* that goods associated with the human right to welfare will be provided by relevant duty-bearers. In fact, "may" does not imply responsibility; it simply implies permissibility. Once again, the global poor may be excluded from claiming the human right to welfare if we ground it in interdependence.

Third, deciding who deserves assistance based on who we interact with is impractical. If we ground human rights in interdependence, the decision to consider someone part of an interdependent network will be occasion specific and will be open to interpretation as to who qualifies for assistance. By arguing that interdependence is based on *relevant* interactions – formal political or economic relationships – we leave interdependence open to interpretation and ultimately misuse. Distinguishing between relevant and irrelevant interactions is also practically burdensome because it forces policymakers to consider who is a part of an interdependent network during a controversial emergency. If an earthquake has occurred in North Korea, the decision to act must not be held up by a conversation about whether we actually have a connection with North Koreans or not. Assurances of welfare cannot be occasion-specific. Likewise, because a type of aid required is time-sensitive, its delivery must not be held up whilst policy makers decide the degree to which a certain country has a "relevant" interaction.

So, grounding the human right to welfare in interdependence and recognising our interconnectedness implies that we have a duty to all humans with whom we have interactions. However, grounding human rights in interdependence is problematic because it does not account for people in isolated communities and it perpetuates global inequalities and injustice. Additionally, determinations of which countries or people exist outside global systems can be situation-specific or inflicted on outlier states. If, then, even when rights are said to be grounded in interdependence, we still provide assistance, there must be a stronger, universal grounding at the heart of human rights. For discussion of this grounding I now turn to the humanity-based grounding of human rights.

4.3.3 Humanity-based grounding of human rights

In this section, I explain a third way of grounding the human right to welfare – the humanity-based approach. After putting the idea of shared humanity in context, I explain how the humanity-based approach to human rights can be understood either in terms of membership of the human species or in terms of the "unique" features we share as humans. I defend the view that human beings are inherently valuable and thus are deserving of respect. I then discuss why humanity-based grounding is the most appropriate grounding of human rights.

An example will help set the scene. There are tribes deep in the Amazon that have not had contact with the world beyond their villages. One such tribe exists in the state of Acre. This tribe may have had contact with outsiders at some point but mainly they have lived a completely isolated existence (Survival, 2014). This means that, until very recently, the tribe did not have any economic or social interactions with the rest of humankind. Integration of this tribe into global society is unnecessary.

Now, consider a situation in which a forest fire is quickly spreading toward the tribe. The fire was not started by humans but it is within human control to stop the fire. Ethically, many of us would think that saving the members of this tribe would still be the right thing to do. Do these individuals have the right to our assistance? I have argued in this chapter that pain and suffering and interdependence (or lack thereof) are not sufficient to require international assistance. However, one response to the question I have posed is that we should save the people of Acre because they are humans.

It should be noted that the human right to welfare can be grounded in humanity in two different ways. This right could be argued to be created by either our shared species membership or the "unique features" of human beings. I will discuss these alternatives in turn.

First, any person sharing the same human genetic coding is human – she belongs to the same animal species. By including all genetically identical animals in the definition of humans, we include "marginal humans" (i.e. those with disabilities or limited brain functioning) as well as human children and infants. Accordingly, it could be argued that any Homo sapiens should enjoy human rights simply because she is human.

There are two major objections to grounding human rights in species membership. The first is that doing so privileges a random (though specific) ordering of DNA over that of another being's DNA (Bernstein, 2002, p. 529). The priority placed on humans as deserving of special treatment is speciesist. Singer explains the criticism of species membership as a grounding of human rights as similar to racism or sexism (2003). Hence grounding human rights in species membership is unethical in itself.

Similarly, we do not specify that one race of humans has rights and another does not. This is because all humans have, for example, the same interest in avoiding pain. In fact, when we have empathy for the suffering of humans of different races we are not empathizing with the other, we are empathizing with that which is the same. The morally relevant consideration is a being's interests and avoiding the suffering of that being in contravention of her interests (Singer, 2003; Diamond, 2005/2012). Their interests are our interests; species membership is irrelevant. Hence, grounding human rights on species membership is morally arbitrary in addition to being speciesist.

Chappell explains that often we identify non-humans as "other" first, and then decide how best to apply the criteria of personhood to defend our position (2011). In doing this, we allow for prioritisation of humans because we want humans to be superior, not because they are. By extension we prioritise the interests of humans over other species.[13]

So, the joint humanity grounding of the human right to welfare based on species membership is unacceptable. There is, however, a second way of using the humanity-based grounding. This justification begins from the argument that human beings are unique among beings because there are some unique qualities inherent to human beings that make them valuable. Considering the example of the people of Acre given previously, it can instead be argued that we believe these humans to have a right to assistance based on our common humanity.[14]

The humanity-based grounding of human rights is based on those unique qualities of human beings (Caney, 2010). People disagree about which of the properties are relevant, thus making humans special and deserving of rights. Different arguments exist for which certain properties – sentience, cognition, autonomy, rationality and emotions – are important in this way.

I argue, in line with Griffin, that chief among these qualities is our ability to act autonomously and which seems to set us apart from other beings.[15] Unlike other beings, then, we have the ability to form our own understanding of the good life in critical reflection and to pursue this understanding through intentional action (Griffin, 2000, p. 29, 2008, p. 45).

In contrast, whilst we share other grounding aspects of human rights with non-humans (emotions and sentience), non-human animals do not act on autonomous choices in the same way as we do; they may pursue things that are good for them by instinct but they have not formed their own conception of the good life before they begin to pursue a good life. Because of this, it can be argued that our ability to deliberate and act autonomously is the significant quality that both makes us as human beings unique and deserves to be protected by human rights.

In order to protect our normative agency, that which makes us fully human, Griffin argues that we then need three types of human rights: liberty, autonomy and welfare. Liberty is essentially freedom; no one can stop me from pursuing a good life. Autonomy is self-governance – the ability to make choices about one's own life. Welfare, once again, is minimum provisions. Humans cannot pursue their concept of a good life if they don't have certain basic elements necessary for survival. Hence, liberty, autonomy and welfare are, according to Griffin, the fundamental types of rights which, together, enable humans to live a fully human life as normative agents. By grounding the human right to welfare in "humanity" in this way we are saying that humans can claim the basic material provisions which makes autonomy and liberty, and by extension, a fully human life, possible. (Criticisms of this position are addressed in Section 4.4.)

And so, the uniqueness of humans is the most appropriate way to understand this grounding of human rights. Human rights are protections for us to act as the autonomous agents that we are. This grounding is also consistent with the idea of rights in general because the humanity-based grounding drawn from agency allows for *universal* application – the autonomous agency of each individual person is protected by human rights. Likewise, this grounding is consistent with human rights because it ensures a basic minimum of resources which thus enables to live a good (autonomous) life. And finally, this grounding of the human right to welfare ensures that welfare is a high priority and thus prevents people from inhibiting our own good lives.

The human right to welfare thereby creates a human societal obligation to ensure that those items necessary for survival (food, shelter, medical attention and security) are provided to all humans based on our shared humanity when they are under threat.

4.4 Criticisms of human rights use in policymaking

There are various criticisms of human rights, though, which should be addressed considering the centrality of human rights to my argument. Traditional utilitarians argue that human rights are simply "nonsense upon stilts" and thus should not be used to justify any policy (Bentham, 2002). Social contract theorists may argue that there are certain rights only deliverable by the state in which a person lives. Similarly, libertarians may argue that the rights argued for herein are actually negative rights and hence a duty to provide the goods in question does not exist. I discuss and respond to each of these criticisms of human rights in turn.

4.4.1 Utilitarian argument

First, utilitarians make two arguments against using rights as the foundation of policymaking. The first argument pertains to the existence of rights in general. The second argument considers the existence of a human right to welfare in particular.

On the existence of rights, Bentham argues that human rights do not exist and hence cannot and should not be used to ground policies and practice of any kind (Bentham, 2002). In responding to the establishment of the French Declaration of Rights, Bentham argued that the idea of "rights" of man was empty and highly problematic. For example, he argued that the human right to liberty cannot be grounded in reality because, as a matter of fact, humans are not free. All men are not born free and hence any reference to the inherent rights of humans prior to the existence of a state (i.e. rights stemming from natural rights) is not grounded in reality (Bentham, 2002, pp. 323–324).[16]

At this point, it could be suggested that natural rights, namely the inherent worth of human beings, underpin human rights. Bentham explains, however, that the French Rights of Man grounded in natural rights "is simple nonsense: natural and imprescriptible rights, rhetorical nonsense, nonsense upon stilts" (Bentham, 2002, p. 330). Articulation of rights is only an articulation of a need and one cannot have a duty to preserve an abstract need. Instead, rights are more appropriately understood as a legal construct, grounded in national structures. There cannot realistically be moral rights because there is no basis upon which to ground them, or so Bentham argued.

I disagree with Bentham's argument that rights are simply rhetorical devices, not grounded in reality, and that even speaking of them can lead to anarchy. The main problem of his "rhetorical devices" claim is that a grounding for human rights can indeed be found in reality. As explained previously, human rights can be grounded in the fact that human beings are normative agents

– they are able to form independent conceptions of a good life and pursue it. Rousseau famously argues that men are, indeed, born free. Only from societal "convention" are humans restricted in this freedom to make claims for themselves. Likewise, though, through these conventions men can pursue the return of said freedom (Rousseau, 1998). Hence, there is a ground for human rights in the way things are.

Importantly, human rights are articulations of what normative agents *should* be entitled to and in this way are normative. What Bentham's discussion misses is that rights are inherently normative: they explain what claims people should be able to make on society. Rights are not set out as descriptive notions of the lives humans currently live – they are claims on the lives we should be living. In this way, we cannot rely on legal systems to ensure our rights. If we do, humans will be left open to the subjective, prejudicial and changeable nature of policy, politics and politicians.

My second issue with Bentham's argument about rights is that he suggests that rights are dangerous because they can lead to anarchy. If rights do not spring from national laws, then governments will constantly be open to revolution and anarchy, or so he claimed (Alexander, 2003, p. 11; Bentham, 2002). The central concern here seems to be that a governmental authority will be questioned or overturned should the people feel they are not receiving what is owed them. Alexander suggests that Bentham is concerned that rights form a "foundation of political legitimacy on a utopian, unachievable fiction" (2003, p. 11).

Whilst complete and universal adherence to universal human rights norms has not been achieved (and many countries still violate human rights), the perpetuation of human rights norms since the 1950s has not caused anarchy. Despite revolutionary overthrows of governments linked to demands for the goods associated with human rights, we do not live in anarchy. Actually, governments have been overthrown for centuries before people accepted that they had human rights. In this way, human rights are not particularly at odds with a national government's peaceful rule over a territory.

Furthermore, other than the possibility of violence or hardship for those concerned, I do not see why a government being responsible to its people for some moral reasons is so controversial. I would argue that there should be a moral mechanism for people to make demands of their government. As will be discussed in Chapter 8, legitimacy depends not simply on citizens following laws and acquiescing to authority. Indeed, the state must also uphold a moral norm within the society based on duties to its people.

The second utilitarian argument against using human rights as the foundation of policymaking has to do with a specific understanding of welfare maximisation. There is a conflict between rights theory and utilitarianism. It can be argued on utilitarian grounds that in some instances welfare will need to be re-distributed (taken from one, given to another) in order to maximise societal well-being. Consider a transplant case here and that there are three people in need of different organs. If one healthy person walks into the hospital (and in the absence of other moral questions), welfare maximisation in line with the above entails that it would be morally permissible to kill that one person for her organs in order to maximise overall welfare (Thomson, 1976; Sinnott-Armstrong, 2015). Realistically, no one would make the moral argument for killing one to save three. In this way, developing policy based on human rights is more appropriate.

4.4.2 Social contract argument

A second possible criticism of human rights is related to social contract theory. According to contractarians there is a social contract between citizens and government which only exists at the national level. This contract is an ongoing and consistently re-assessed agreement: "Each of us puts in common his person and his whole power under the supreme direction of the general will; and in return we receive, every member as an indivisible part of the whole" (Rousseau, 1998). Together, something larger than oneself is formed which ensures the preservation of our rights. In Section 4.3.2, I outlined the interdependence-based grounding of the human right to welfare which includes a more thorough argument against that of the contractarians. The duty to provide certain rights, it is argued, is only deliverable by the government with which an individual has engaged in such a contract. Within the terms of the social contract theory and assuming that certain rights (i.e. welfare) are a civic right, it can be argued that it is up to the state to provide for its citizens.[17] Human rights are therefore excessive; rights are maintained at the state level and spreading the associated responsibilities to *all* humans is unnecessary.[18]

Now, the social contract criticism of human rights would suggest that developing policy for distinct communities may be a worthwhile venture. However, this assumes that each bounded territory represents a distinct civilisation (Waldron, 1987, p. 169). In fact, countries are multicultural and diverse communities in which there will be many people who did not enter into the social contract with the state in which they live. It follows that the needs of certain people within a country will not be afforded the same rights as offered to their contractarian neighbours. Human rights account for diverse communities and ensure equal and universal enforcement of the scope of certain rights. To ensure that all people within a state receive equal enjoyment of rights, there must actually be human rights; rights at the state level are not enough.

4.4.3 Libertarian argument

A third possible critique of human rights is grounded in libertarian norms. In a libertarian view, governments only have *negative duties* not to harm. Most importantly, the burden positive rights cause would inhibit individual negative liberty (Cross, 2001, p. 863). I should be free to use my money and my time to pursue a good life for myself. *Positive duties*, in contrast, would require government assistance in response to individuals' claims (Cross, 2001). That would require me to spend my time and money on someone else's desires and needs.

Indeed, according to libertarians there are no positive duties. Any positive rights and associated duties would likely be politically and economically cumbersome. Additionally, a positive right requires that a governmental system exists (at whatever level) to fulfil the associated duties (Cross, 2001, p. 866). This would restrict the liberty of individuals; only constraints like time, nature, and ability (things that cannot be controlled) should limit a person's pursuit of their own good life. So, libertarians argue that no one should interfere with personal freedom (freedom being the thing that allows a person to pursue a flourishing life as they see it) and by extension they would argue against the existence of a human right to welfare.[19]

The libertarian view is problematic. Welfare and freedom are both important for the same reason: they both enable a person to pursue a good life. However, we should also note that, without basic welfare (food, water, shelter and medical assistance), a person cannot interact with or enjoy their freedom and thus not freely act on their pursuit of a flourishing life. For example, I should be free to own property and manage a given piece of land in a way that will add to my own good life. If I choose to farm the land so that I am self-sufficient but then break my arm and no one is able to manage my farm for me, I will not have any food and no recourse to assistance. Surely, a good life would entail access to food. If libertarians think that freedom matters, they should likewise recognise that a right to basic welfare will equally enable them to basic food stuffs which will enable them to pursue their own idea of a good life. Hence, welfare is at least as important as liberty in supporting a person's pursuit of a good life.

In sum, there are various critics of the concept of a universal human rights structure. Libertarians, social contract theorists and utilitarians propose reasoned criticism of the development and application of human rights to policy making. However, human rights are an appropriate type of right in that they are universal, treat individuals equally, and ensure that the goods associated with certain rights are provided to right-holders.

4.5 Conclusion

I have explained that human rights are a particular kind of right. There are three features of human rights pertinent to my argument: they are high priority norms, set minimum standards and are universal. Welfare is the human right focused on in this chapter and the wider book. There are at least three ways to understand welfare: hedonism, desire-satisfaction and objective-list theories. In this chapter, I argued for objective-list theories of welfare because it is consistent with human rights in general and helps to establish the human right to welfare as a high priority norm, set a universal standard (for the provision of welfare) and, the objective list means that it can be universally applied. Items like food, water, shelter and medical care set a minimum standard for what is necessary for survival and ultimately contribute to one's ability to lead a good life. The human right to welfare grounded in the uniqueness of humans based on our agency and ability to know and act on our own idea of a good life is the most convincing grounding because it is consistent with the spirit of rights, allows for universal application, and is the most practically implemented.

In sum, human rights are an appropriate mechanism around which policy should be made. Looking forward to my development of natural hazard and disaster intervention policy, human rights are the appropriate mechanism to justify the need for such policy because the human right to welfare accounts for the basic needs of all humans. Furthermore, the human right to welfare is a high priority norm and is of a higher priority than other national-level political or economic rights. Additionally, the human right to welfare sets the minimum standard as to the provision of basic goods and forces the universal provision of such goods in line with the normative function of human rights.

Notes

1 Beitz argues that human rights cannot be understood as timeless: as science and technology change, our duties to humans also change (2003, pp. 43–44). However, human rights are normative and represent the ideal of human society. Hence I argue that whilst our technology and science may change it does not mean that our respect for humans will or should change.
2 Some rights theorists such as Henry Shue argue that minimum standards help to ensure that human life does not sink below a minimal standard necessary for survival (1980). By dictating only minimal standards, national governments can maintain and integrate human rights into national laws with relative ease; this means that national governments are free to administer and implement political and social laws which fits the needs of the country without conflicting with human rights (Nickel, 2017).
3 As high priority norms, human rights are also the standard bearer against which the international community evaluates the political legitimacy of different states. We judge their legitimacy on whether a state kills its own people (Robinson, 2007, p. 87). When a state does not carry out this function of protecting the basic rights of citizens it is not legitimate. Hence, human rights are of the highest priority for states as duty bearer as well as for the individuals making claims.
4 See also Nussbaum (1999, p. 229).
5 Whilst objective lists often combine elements of desire-satisfaction and hedonism (in that some items on an objective list do bring us pleasure and fulfil our desires) it does not solely concern things that fulfil desires or are pleasurable (Crisp, 2016; Fletcher, 2013).
6 The international community has second-order responsibilities because they too can ensure certain rights but should wait for the state to act first (Caney, 2014, p. 134; Euro-Atlantic Partnership Council, 1998; IFRC, 2016, p. 165).
7 By its very nature, the human right to welfare establishes a basic minimum of those goods necessary for survival. According to Masolw's hierarchy of needs any human need "rests on the prior satisfaction of another pre-potent need" (1943). Basic needs are the most important and most fundamental to human existence such that they take priority over all other needs and desires (Maslow, 1943). Once the basic needs of food, water and shelter are satisfied, one can attempt to satisfy other needs and desires (see Cross, 2001).
8 Robinson argues that a state may still be legitimate even if the entire citizenry does not support it; a majority of the citizens should not be opposed to its continuing to govern. He also argues that a legitimate state must protect the basic rights of its citizens and refrain from violating the rights of those in other

states. When these functions are not upheld, intervention may be possible (2007, p. 87).

9 Singer argues that all members of the moral community deserve not to suffer or feel pain when it can be prevented. I limit my argument to humans for purpose of space and focus within this text.

10 Singer argued that distance does not authorise us to ignore pain and suffering (1972, p. 232). Practical limitations, such as distance which prevents timely response, do exist. Hence, whilst distance may not be a moral limitation, it may be a practical one.

11 Institutional cosmopolitanism is the view that all humans are co-*citizens* of the world and thus share political and judicial structures. Accordingly, and in line with an interdependence-based view of human rights, humans linked as co-citizens belong to a political community thus engaging them in a type of social contract (Ronzoni, 2013). Simon Caney explains that an interdependence-based cosmopolitanism would require distributive justice to all members of the global institutional structure. Those outside the structures, however, could only claim rights to humanitarian assistance, not to justice more broadly (2009).

12 This is not, I would argue, to do with duty to co-humans but rather a lack of political will.

13 A second criticism to using species membership as the qualifier for membership in humanity involves the issue of reproduction, though it is unnecessary to unpack here (Bernstein, 2002).

14 This grounding is consistent with the universality and equality of both rights and duties. It is also consistent with cosmopolitan justice which stresses the importance of individuals.

15 Nonhuman animals can be said to feel pain and pleasure, rationality and emotions and thus do not provide an explanation of what makes humans unique and therefore deserving of rights.

16 Bentham further argued that humans are not equal in rights. To say so is to ignore the existence of privilege and power in the world (Bentham, 2002, p. 325). Likewise, socialists can claim that the scope of rights is still entrenched in issues of class and power (Waldron, 1987, p. 159). Liberals suggest that rights do not adequately account for the needs of a given society. By focusing on helping the individual we may not support society in such a way as to make the individual's life, within that society, meaningful (Waldron, 1987, p. 158). Consider, for example, that rights are not universal; the oppression of rights suffered by men are only a component of greater and separate oppressions suffered by women (Waldron, 1987, p. 159).

17 Indeed the social contract legitimates the state and allows it to govern with the consent of the citizens. For more on a recent, Rawlsian explanation of social contract theory see (Nussbaum, 2007, pp. 4–5).

18 I will respond to this criticism thoroughly in Chapter 7.

19 It problematically follows that human rights are not something to be delivered by the international community to individuals (Pogge, 2008, p. 70). The state's role is solely to ensure that individuals are free to pursue their own interests without external interference. I expect, though, that if assistance was offered by a national (or supranational) government, libertarians would not refuse life-saving support.

5 Case study

International response to Cyclone Nargis (Myanmar)

As explained, I am concerned with avoidable human suffering after the occurrence of natural hazards. This focus is meant to motivate an international perspective and response in the aftermath of a natural hazard when national governments are unable or unwilling to discharge their duties. I argue that preparedness must involve the development of a safety net for the humans affected in the event that a national government is in fact unable or unwilling to respond. In making this argument, I must first make the case that a safety net does not exist.

In this chapter, I begin with an explanation of the type of events in question and set the scene for arguments in favour of military intervention made in later chapters. The definition of a disaster resulting from a natural hazard I gave in Chapter 1 is as follows: a social disruption or impact triggered by a phenomenon of the physical world, usually weather-related, which is sudden-onset and affects a population. In Section 5.1, I explain the various phases of disaster response and recovery in general terms. In Section 5.2, I explain the particulars associated with the response to Cyclone Nargis.

5.1 The phases of disaster response

In order to more easily enable the allocation of resources and responsibilities, facilitate measurement and otherwise practical concerns, the phases of a disaster are often broken down into preparedness, response, recovery and mitigation. These usually follow in succession but a disaster response may not pass through one or more of these phases. Recovery from a disaster is not, as Neal explains, "a simple, linear, or cyclical process" (1997, p. 244). It is a chaotic operation which must adapt to often conflicting needs and demands. Accordingly, it may not be realistic to split disaster response into "phases" for they are not "discrete units" of measurement (Neal, 1997, p. 254). Likewise there is no general consensus as to when one phase has come to an end and another has started.[1] That said, talking about phases of disaster response are practically useful.

First, a note on resilience. We cannot prevent all natural hazards from occurring; hence we cannot outright prevent the disaster that results. We can mitigate a disaster's impact by building global resilience to natural hazards and the resultant disasters (IFRC, 2016).[2] Indeed, the UNISDR calls for an "ethic of prevention" in our dealings with natural hazards such that we can reduce overall damage caused by a trigger event (such as an earthquake, hurricane, tornado, etc.) (UNISDR, 2017). Preparing and responding to a natural hazard are underpinned by an ethos of resilience, the aim of which is to reduce the impact of disasters (UNISDR, 2015). It is broadly accepted that we reduce the impact of disasters by improving societal conditions; by doing so we minimise a community's vulnerability (and hence risk) (Shea, 2016; European Commission, 2012; IFRC, 2016). This, by extension, reduces the possible impact that a disaster will have on a specific community.

I move now to discussing the specific phases of response particular to natural hazards. These include preparedness, response, post-response and reconstruction. First on preparedness, we prepare for disasters because it is important to prevent suffering when we can. Preparedness plans often establish what a basic level of welfare looks like, and how that can be maintained or re-established in the event of a disaster. Additionally, preparedness measures provide an opportunity to save lives and money and may put off the need for future interventions (Fixdal & Smith, 1998, p. 302). Accordingly, maximising preparedness will help to minimise the amount of response assistance needed. Under many current regulations, prevention and relief (which often includes response and recovery) are actually the only way to ensure that all support that can be given to affected people is given. For example, the Hyogo Framework for Action, a platform for international cooperation on disaster risk reduction, has listed preparedness as one of the top five priorities for international disaster response planning (International Strategy for Disaster Reduction, 2008). Likewise, the *Draft Articles on the Protection of Persons in the Event of Disasters* require national governments to ensure that all legal provisions relating to the acceptance and integration of external assistance are in place ahead of a disaster (United Nations, 2016).

Furthermore, preparedness helps to ensure the welfare of those affected. For example, the US preparedness goal stresses the importance of "whole community" preparedness (DHS, 2015). A "whole community" includes all individuals and groups in addition to government and is to be a "shared responsibility" (DHS, 2015). With proper planning we can aim at a policy which Zack refers to as "Save the Greatest Number with the Best Preparation Possible" (2011). Through this approach to preparedness, decisions can be made with the appropriate consideration and it is possible to save more people than would have had a plan of action not been in place. This will help to reduce the amount of time wasted and avoid overzealous use force in support of those plans. So, the best way to provide for human welfare is to prepare ahead of a natural hazard.

I now move on to discuss the other response phases. The period immediately following the hazard event, during which the life-saving operations take place, is usually referred to as the "response" phase. After response, operations may transition into a "reconstruction phase" or "recovery phase", depending on the type of operations carried out. It should be noted that in disaster response there is not a static time period delineating the response and recovery phases (Neal, 1997). Response and recovery elements are often mixed and depend on the disaster's specific dynamics as well as the social situation affected (Neal, 1997, p. 249). This all supports the premise that disaster phases are used for practical purposes and should not be understood temporally (Neal, 1997, p. 259). I do not discuss "mitigation" phase as it occurs only after all life-saving and life-sustaining assistance has been carried out and thus is superfluous to my argument.

5.2 Myanmar (Burma)

Cyclone Nargis struck Myanmar in 2008. The damage and impact of the cyclone inspired controversy as to the need for natural hazard intervention, I include this case study because it offers evidence of a government unwilling to respond to the needs of its people in the aftermath of a natural hazard. Additionally, this scenario provides a reasonable baseline for future discussion as to when intervention may be appropriate (see also Barber, 2009).

After the violent government response to pro-democracy demonstrations in 1988, the US Mission to Burma closed in 1989 citing wide-scale human rights abuses (Human Rights Watch, 1989; US Department of State, 2016). Upon assuming power, the Burmese generals changed the country's name to Myanmar (JF, 2016). Following what many described as a "massacre" of pro-democracy campaigners by the Burmese Army, foreign governments suspended economic aid programmes to Myanmar (Human Rights Watch, 1989). Soon thereafter, the government ignored its own pledges to hold open and fair elections. The generals then went on to ignore the overwhelming support for pro-democracy candidate Aung San Suu Kyi. She was arrested and placed under house arrest on various occasions (and for years at a time) from 1989 to 2010 (Beake, 2019; Human Rights Watch, 1989; NobelPrize.org, 1991). Since the generals rise to power, the US government cited multiple reports of their failure to support workers' rights, mistreatment of prisoners, and the torture of ethnic minorities and others held in detention (Human Rights Watch, 1989). Over the years the political situation in Myanmar has become increasingly inimical to democracy and human rights.

The Myanmar case highlights multiple failings which have hindered assistance reaching those individuals affected by a natural hazard in a hostile state. This case was also chosen because it represents a counter-argument to my central argument in this book and can hence be used to assess whether a policy development may be necessary.

In 2008, Cyclone Nargis tested the country's ability and willingness to respond to the needs of its entire population – not just those friendly to and/or favoured by the regime. However, by assuming control of the sovereign state, the government of Myanmar entered into a compact with its citizens to provide for their needs in an emergency. One way in which it can defend its legitimacy to govern is through providing emergency care (Ozerdem, 2010, p. 698). I now proceed to explaining a situation in which Myanmar's legitimacy was questioned during an emergency situation.[3]

5.2.1 Impact of Cyclone Nargis

On 2 May 2008, Cyclone Nargis struck off the west coast of Myanmar as a Category 4 storm (IFRC, 2011). Winds blew at around 130 mph and by 3 May the storm had damaged or destroyed 800,000 private buildings and ultimately left around 1million people homeless (Asian Development Bank, 2008). Death estimates range from 85,000 to 140,000 due to the Cyclone and a total of 2.4 million were affected in some way or another (IFRC, 2011). The national government was 'overwhelmed' by the scale of the disaster and any available and pre-positioned supplies were quickly depleted (The Association of Southeast Asian Nations, 2009).

As in any natural hazard, as the storm passed and people were able to reach out to aid agencies and responders, the true impact of the storm became clear. By 5 May, international aid agencies and various governments were readying their response operations in support of the Burmese people. On Haing Gyi Island, one of the first areas for Cyclone Nargis to have made landfall, 20,000 homes were destroyed; this resulted in mass homelessness and the pollution of drinking water in the area (The New York Times, 2008). In the Kyaiklat region, known for rice production, 25% of buildings were destroyed (The New York Times, 2008). ASEAN called for member countries to contribute to the obvious disaster relief support required by Myanmar two days into the disaster response (Association of Southeast Asian Nations, 2009).

In the first few days of the response, the government of Myanmar was mainly open to bilateral offers of support (United Nations, 2008).[4] Foreign aid workers already in-country were restricted from moving around the affected area to assess damage (despite their expertise and usual role in similar disaster scenarios elsewhere) (Mydans, 2008). Some experts suggest that assistance was rejected by the Burmese generals because the leaders were apathetic to the suffering of its people; it was said that upholding their sovereign right to rule within the national boundaries seemed to be of utmost importance (Evans, 2008).

5.2.2 (Failed) response phase

After restricting the movement of foreign aid workers and hindering their work, the international community and the government of Myanmar entered talks to discuss the possibility of foreign assistance being allowed into the country. However, the Myanmar government rejected any assistance provided on foreign military vessels (Ozerdem, 2010, p. 698). It also stopped granting visas to foreign aid workers (Mydans, 2008). Meanwhile, US diplomats estimated that the death toll from starvation, exposure to the elements and disease would rise to 100,000 without foreign intervention (Mydans, 2008).

By 7 May 2008, some in the international community, most notably the French Foreign Minister Bernard Kouchner, suggested that the UN invoke the Responsibility to Protect doctrine and mobilise an intervention in response to Cyclone Nargis (Alertnet, 2008). Kouchner invoked the priority of human rights, the original driver behind the Responsibility to Protect doctrine, to trigger intervention into Myanmar. The French further suggested that the United States should intervene without the permission of the military junta managing both the country and the supposed cyclone response (Mydans, 2008). By intervening, timely food and first aid supplies would likely reach those in need.

French Ambassador to the UN Ripert argued that the national government's denial of aid into the country in a timely and suitable manner could constitute a "crime against humanity" (Ozerdem, 2010, p. 699). On 13 May, internal European Union discussions suggested that all possible EU action should be taken; the UK government indicated that air drops of aid were one possible course of action (Belanger & Horsey, 2008). An independent report on the post-disaster actions of the government of Myanmar found that the generals were actively blocking this and other international aid and suggested that the government be referred to the International Criminal Court for crimes against humanity (MacKinnon, 2009). Hence international action was deemed necessary by those arguing for the invocation of RtoP. Likewise, international intervention was preferred as the invocation of sanctions would likely risk long-term economic instability in the country.

One argument against intervening in Myanmar was that the situation did not create "a threat to international peace and security" and as such no action was called for by the United Nations (ICRtoP, n.d.). Other experts suggested that an intervention would not be a guarantee that assistance would reach those affected. Likewise, an intervention would have possibly risked making a natural hazard into a political dilemma and thus risked political instability for the country (Ozerdem, 2010, p. 701). Long-term instability would also mean that human welfare would be hindered by long-term political instability (possibly conflict) triggered by international intervention (see Section 6.3). Additionally, the international community had to weigh the impending death of Burmese citizens against the country's sovereignty. Gareth Evans further argued that any intervention for a cause not originally agreed to under the terms of RtoP would undermine RtoP in general and any future invocation to assist those suffering from mass atrocity (2008).

Conversations amongst the international community continued despite calls for an intervention. Eventually, after 11 days without assistance and after extensive negotiations, foreign assistance was accepted from ASEAN. Because ASEAN is a local cooperative organisation, acceptance of assistance helped Myanmar save face amidst pushes for it to accept aid more widely. Finally, on 23 May, extensive negotiation between the UN and the Myanmar government resulted in an agreement that international assistance would be allowed into the country (Belanger & Horsey, 2008). A forcible intervention was therefore no longer necessary. If negotiation with the Burmese generals had not gone the way it did after Cyclone Nargis, there is a possibility that the international community would have intervened with military force.

I have chosen to focus on Cyclone Nargis for several reasons. First, this is a relatively recent disaster and the details are part of a debate still in active memory. It is easier to understand the impact and the necessary response to future disasters, if we can still remember what happened the last time. Second, the Burmese generals' refusal of assistance provides actual evidence that a government may be unwilling to accept assistance or provide assistance for its own people. Finally, the possibility of military intervention when natural hazard assistance is refused is likewise part of recent debate.

5.3 Conclusion

In this chapter, I have described how a national government did not always play the robust and central role in disaster response that it should have. I set out the phases of a disaster response so as to help the reader make sense of the real-world scenario offered in this chapter. The case study used was that of the response to Cyclone Nargis in Myanmar in 2008. Myanmar's response provides a real example of a government unwilling to provide for the needs of its people in the aftermath of a natural hazard and hence offers background to the discussion of "why we should intervene" to which we now turn.

Notes

1 In fact, agreement about what constitutes a disaster cycle in one culture may be something completely different in another; likewise, individual perception about what is a disaster matters (Neal, 1997, p. 256).
2 As per the Sendai Framework Agreement, states are required to develop and implement Disaster Risk Reduction initiatives (UNISDR, 2015, p. 13). This requires a "multi-hazard approach". Hence any suggestions I make about responding to "natural" hazards should be seen as a component part of a larger, all-hazards approach to disaster risk.
3 For further discussion of this topic in light of sovereignty-related objections to natural hazard intervention, see Chapter 8.
4 The national government's duty to protect affected citizens and provide relief assistance was formalised into international doctrine in 2016 (United Nations, 2016). Furthermore, the Articles on the Protection of Persons in the Event of Disasters further specify that an affected country must take the "necessary measures, within its national law, to facilitate the prompt and effective provision of external assistance" (United Nations, 2016, Art. 15). Whilst this doctrine has been formalised after the Myanmar incident, these are standard humanitarian norms and expectations of behaviour and hence would have existed de facto if not de jure.

6 Why we should intervene for natural hazard response

In Chapter 3, I discussed the current norms of intervention, which state that intervention is a possible means of international response when there is drastic risk to human life or when international peace and security is threatened. However, current norms of intervention only count genocide, large-scale human rights abuse, humanitarian emergencies and war crimes as possible triggers for intervention. Hence a caveat to the intervention norm is that it is only permissible in specific situations; natural hazards are specifically excluded. Accordingly, natural hazard military intervention is impermissible according to current standards, it does not occur and policy to support such interventions does not exist.

In this chapter, I show that interventions in natural hazard scenarios are morally permissible and morally required in some cases. Because of this, international natural hazard intervention policy that addresses these moral requirements should be developed. For the purposes of making this argument, I use the Cyclone Nargis case study from Chapter 5.

In Section 6.1, I explain what the current international policies of intervention would say about intervening in the Cyclone Nargis scenario, when a government is unwilling to respond to its own domestic disaster. I carry out the same analysis for when a government is unable to respond and/or allow in foreign assistance in the second half of that section. In Section 6.2, I outline problems with the status quo and how current international laws and norms do not universally account for the rights of humans. In Section 6.3, given my analysis of the human right to welfare and international laws and norms, intervention is actually an appropriate response method to natural hazards in specific scenarios. I proceed with this argument by explaining once again why the human right to welfare is important, how it should apply in natural hazard scenarios (for example in the Myanmar case) and finally, why an intervention should be defended on these grounds.

In the Cyclone Nargis situation, NGOs were, in essence, hindered from providing assistance to the Burmese people. That would have been bad enough but the generals themselves were not delivering aid to citizens either. As Caney suggests, and this case evidences, states may be incompetent, negligent, or simply not doing what they are supposed to do (2013, p. 155). Only after extensive negotiation were foreign counterparts able to persuade the generals to allow necessary supplies into the country.

6.1 Current laws and standards

As outlined previously, the precise circumstances in which the international community is permitted to intervene in a sovereign nation are governed by international law. Using Cyclone Nargis as an example, I first discuss the laws which apply to governments unwilling to request/consent to assistance in the aftermath of a natural hazard as happened after Cyclone Nargis. Second, I discuss the laws and norms that would apply in a similar emergency scenario but where government officials are simply unable to request or consent to assistance from the international community. I outline the problems with accepting these laws and norms as they currently exist.

First, according to the current laws and norms, intervention for natural hazard relief is not allowed in situations in which a government is unwilling to support its citizens or to consent to international offers of assistance. The United Nations Charter provides the clearest reasons against interventions in these cases. According to Chapter VII of the UN Charter, force can only be used in situations that constitute a threat to international peace. Likewise, Article 2(7) stipulates that nothing in the UN Charter allows for intervention into the domestic affairs of another state (Massingham, 2009, p. 812). Notably, a natural hazard intervention norm which accounts for the stipulations of the UN Charter yet allows for intervention – like the norm of RtoP – does not exist. Instead, the rules outlined by the UN Charter set a precedent and deter any interventions of the kind suggested in this section. When applied to a Cyclone Nargis situation, those who argue that intervention is inappropriate could argue that any use of force would violate international law.

Furthermore, RtoP cannot be used to justify intervention in natural hazard cases because none of the doctrine's conditions necessitating intervention have been met. The government of Myanmar did not commit genocide and accordingly there is no threat to international peace and security. There is, therefore, no reason to invoke RtoP (see Section 3.2.3). Remember, natural hazards are purposely excluded from RtoP because they would require political will beyond that garnered in the original discussions and because adding relief for natural hazards to the list of triggers for RtoP would be too onerous for the interveners.

In sum, if we take current doctrine, the situation of those who have been affected by a Cyclone Nargis situation is not grounds for intervention according to international standards. Action by the international community is not allowed because none of the accepted grounds for intervention – genocide, large-scale human rights abuse, humanitarian emergencies, disruptions to international peace and security – have been met.

I move now to discussion of a case where instead of being unwilling to respond, a national government is unable to respond. This would mean that a national government is not logistically or operationally able to provide for the needs of its citizens. (Consider the situation in Haiti in the aftermath of the 2010 earthquake.)[1] I am purposely ignoring national laws and policies on how to respond to a natural hazard. I am assuming that an inability to respond means that response must be elevated beyond the state to some other (non-national) authority.

According to UNGA Resolution 46/182, a national government has a primary duty to its citizens to provide for "the initiation, organization, coordination, and implementation of humanitarian assistance within its territory" in the event of a natural hazard (United Nations General Assembly, 1991). Also, according to international human rights law, a national government has a duty to provide the basic goods that are essential for survival. When a national government is unable to provide the essentials to its affected citizens, it is then required to request assistance from the international community (Harper, 2009).

In this situation, where the delivery of those items which come under the scope of the human right to welfare is in question, there is a role for the international community. At the very least, the international community has a duty to support a national government where possible (United Nations General Assembly, 1991). The international community has established guidelines intended to minimise regulatory issues involved with the integration of foreign assistance into a domestic emergency and has established teams available for deployment should a national government require such assistance (UN General Assembly Economic and Social Council, 2003). The re-establishment of the national government apparatus is paramount to appropriate national hazard response as is supporting the human rights of those affected. Accordingly, a "swift return to law and order" will help facilitate national adherence to their duties to those affected as mandated by the Universal Declaration of Human Rights (Harper, 2009, p. 28). In sum, the international community is at least operationally prepared to provide the requested assistance to the affected country should such assistance be requested.

However, I am assuming that the government is unable to request assistance even if the need for this assistance still exists. The re-establishment of law and order and the support to human rights assumes that aid agencies will be working in concert with, and with the consent of, the national government (Harper, 2009). However, without a request for assistance, there is no operational or legal mechanism through which the international community could respond. Even if the political will for supporting emergency response existed in this scenario, there would be no way for the international community to act without the explicit consent of the national government. This is the central problem of the current standards: explicit consent is required despite the fact that national and local institutions may have been destroyed or the official decision makers may have perished.

6.2 Problems with the status quo

In considering problems with the status quo of laws and provisions available for post-natural hazard intervention, I analyse legal and normative practices which guide disaster relief operations and suggest ways in which the moral shortcomings of such practices stand in the way of effective provision of post-natural hazard assistance. The issues to be discussed include the non-binding nature of international law, the standard procedures which are only utilised when consent is available, assumptions that natural hazard assistance will always be delivered in "times of peace", and ultimately the lack of an effective mechanism for intervention on behalf of suffering humans.

First, the relevant laws and standards on the provision of humanitarian relief which guide the international community are non-binding. For example, the Interagency Standing Committee (IASC) *Operational Guidelines on Human Rights and Natural Disasters* and the *Guiding Principles on Internal Displacement* set out the rights of those affected by a disaster and guidance for those who have the corresponding duties to deliver on these rights at the national level (OCHA, 2004; IASC, 2006). However, there is no mechanism which requires (with risk of punishment) a state to uphold either its human rights obligations or its duties to provide for its citizens in the aftermath of a natural hazard in line with these protocols. Additionally, there is no legal requirement to adhere to these guidelines (Harper, 2009, p. 26). With no legal requirement, and no international doctrine or norm for the enforcement of such duties in the event of a natural hazard, states are not bound to provide natural hazard relief to their own people.

Second, there are standards and operating procedures which are triggered should humanitarian relief be required but only when a government has consented. Humanitarian relief is normally facilitated through the Emergency Relief Coordinator, who obtains consent from the affected government and negotiates operational requirements and security plans. When consent has been granted the delivery of assistance will be done in line with the principles of neutrality, impartiality and independence (as per Security Resolution 1894).[2] This ensures that those delivering aid as well as those receiving it can do so in relative safety (UNOCHA, 2014).

However, these rules are problematic because the delivery of relief requires that the affected country has consented, despite the normative position that "humanitarian action should be based on assessed need and provided to all persons affected by the natural disaster without adverse distinction of any kind other than that of different needs" (IASC Principle B.1.2) (Harper, 2009, p. 36). Indeed, the international community maintains that all persons affected by a natural hazard should receive equal assistance without distinction. This suggests that the international community is not prepared to officially prioritise those needs over the sovereign right of a national government to consent to assistance. So, laws, policies or mechanisms for intervention that would govern situations in which a government is unable to provide assistance to its people and are, at the same time, unable to provide consent for the international community's involvement, do not currently exist.

Third, the status quo of natural hazard response assumes the conditions set out in the Oslo Guidelines and hence military force will only be used for natural around emergencies during "times of peace" (Multinational, 2007). Intervention without consent of the affected government would thus be paramount to an invasion.[3] As it stands, then, current international doctrine suggests that there will simply not be a situation in which a natural hazard requires assistance in a non-peaceful environment.

If a national government has consented to assistance then of course the acceptance and integration of foreign military assets into a domestic response will be done peacefully through disaster relief mechanisms. However, this "peace time" thinking ignores Myanmar-type situations (or where a government has been completely destroyed) where consent to assistance is not forthcoming but the assistance is still required in support of the human right to welfare. If assistance was forced on the Myanmar government in those early days it would have been without the consent of a national government and thus would have bypassed (indeed, ignored) the national government. This intervention would have been met with force and interveners would have had to respond with force; hence a military component to intervention is necessary.

The use of military in this kind of situation is likely to have contributed to the debate in 2008 and ultimately formed part of the reason the international community did not intervene. I respond to these objections in Section 6.3. I note here, though, that if an intervention (in support of human rights) is required it will be carried out *against* the will of the government (or proxy) and *for* the people affected.[4] Would-be interveners would have taken the side in opposition to the Myanmar national government's authority (in unwilling cases at least). Taking sides means that the international community is no longer neutral and would need to utilise military force as peacekeepers in humanitarian emergencies do. Assistance delivered here would be offered to assist the people directly and does not defer to a national government for consent. Assumptions that such assistance will not require a military component are therefore problematic.

I recognise that assistance delivered with force against the wishes of a non-consenting government or the wishes of those filling a post-emergency power vacuum may be ethically contentious and rails against the status quo of natural hazard relief. However, human rights are of a higher priority than national government consent. Action must be taken with force where necessary to assist affected populations directly.

Indeed, and as I argue, there must be a mechanism for providing assistance (with a military component) when a national government is unable to consent/ask for assistance. The moral requirement to uphold the duties associated with the human right to welfare (as established in Chapter 4) should thereby fall to the international community. Because of this, I argue in future chapters that it is a moral imperative for assistance to be provided (where appropriate as argued for herein) to those affected by a natural hazard regardless of whether consent has been officially granted. Furthermore, I argue that there should be policies for natural hazard military intervention. In the next section, though, I make my argument for why the lack of current laws and standards regarding intervention for natural hazards when a government is unable or unwilling to respond is morally wrong.[5]

6.3 Why we should intervene

Instead of relying on current response plans to provide all necessary assistance post-natural hazard, I argue that military intervention plans should be developed for when – not if – a national government is unable or unwilling to deal with significant domestic disaster response problems. In these cases, a military intervention can act as a failsafe to ensure that adequate assistance is delivered to equally deserving humans. Taking Cyclone Nargis as an example. I argue that when a government is unable or unwilling to provide assistance post-natural hazard a military intervention is in fact morally required. In order to make an argument for interventions in the relevant kind of natural hazard situations, in this section I explain how earlier points made about the human right to welfare and about current norms and laws of intervention made can be used to support the conclusion that international intervention is required in the relevant cases. Specifically, I argue in this section how the human right to welfare requires that we have a mechanism to decide whether to respond.

One of my central claims is that an intervention is morally required when a government's inability or unwillingness to support its citizens threatens human welfare. The human right to welfare makes it so that any person impacted by a natural hazard is entitled to a certain level of welfare regardless of, and independent from, national government policies. Likewise, as a consequence of the right, there is a duty to ensure welfare. National political systems are able to understand what a local population will need in the aftermath of a disaster and be able to implement any required forms of assistance (Shue, 1980, p. 142). National governments thus have first-order duties to provide for the needs (or rather the welfare) of those people affected by a natural hazard. However, as this is a human right to welfare issue and not a political or economic right, the international community has second-order duties to provide for human welfare.

As Griffin explains: "there are some forms of aid that anyone well able to give them owes to anyone in great need of them" (2008, p. 182). When food, shelter and emergency medical care can be given in an emergency, they should be given. Accordingly, as members of the international community (and hence second-order duty-bearers), we must develop policy that not only recognises the importance of welfare but ensures that the goods associated with the right are available to humans in need of those goods. So, as I will argue in this section, if a national government is not delivering on this duty in the aftermath of a natural hazard, intervention may be required.

I first draw from Chapter 4 and remind the reader in Section 6.3.1 why the human right to welfare is so important. In Section 6.3.2, I briefly restate the three possible ways to ground the human right to welfare (from Section 4.3) and then argue that the human right to welfare would be violated in certain natural hazard scenarios if there was no military intervention carried out. In Section 6.3.3, I argue that the human right to welfare morally requires intervention by the international community in the aforementioned kinds of natural hazard scenarios. Finally, in Section 6.3.4 I respond to possible criticisms of my argument.

6.3.1 Human right to welfare is important

First, the human right to welfare is vitally important to our ability to function as autonomous agents. As I argued in Chapter 4, the human right to welfare is a right, it is universal, it sets minimum standards, and it also reflects a high priority moral norm. This right – just like all rights – has its right holders, addressees and a scope.

People affected by natural hazards will need food and water as well as some sort of shelter in the aftermath of a natural hazard. Those affected are entitled to a basic minimum and can claim the required goods from their government. The state government has the corresponding duty to provide the minimum required by those in a disaster situation. With the national government unable or unwilling to support its citizens the normal addressee of the right (the state) fails to carry out its duty to the people. Those affected by an earthquake or tsunami will not be able to be fully autonomous agents and to have a decent human life if they do not have the basic means of survival.

The human right to welfare grounded in our humanity further supports the argument for intervention. When the human right to welfare is grounded in our joint humanity (Section 4.3) – or rather that which makes us unique among sentient beings – it must be guaranteed to all humans, universally. Protection of our normative agency requires that we have necessary basic goods such as food, water, security and health care. Thus when basic goods are not ensured for all humans universally and as the highest priority we can say that a person's rights are being violated.

It follows that in order to be in line with the requirements of human rights, duty-bearers must ensure a basic minimum, universally, and as a high priority to all humans in need of that basic minimum (regardless of their level of pain or relationship with others). If humans affected by a particular natural hazard do not have access to a basic minimum level of welfare, we can say that their rights are being violated. This is cause for action on the part of the international community.

As I explained in Section 2.1.3, disaster relief is a mechanism for providing this basic minimum to those humans struggling to survive in the aftermath of a natural hazard. When offers of disaster relief are ignored, dismissed, or simply not supported, a person's right to basic minimums may also be ignored or dismissed. Accordingly, mechanisms must be established which allow for the provision of a basic minimum in the aftermath of a natural hazard.

6.3.2 The human right to welfare in natural hazard scenarios

The universality of the human right to welfare during natural hazards has often been overlooked. Natural hazards create scenarios in which people cannot enjoy basic levels of well-being. Take Hurricane Katrina (2004), the Haitian Earthquake (2010), and the Boxing Day Tsunami (2004) as examples. With the kinds of devastation present in these scenarios, means of survival are compromised.

The people in any of these natural hazard scenarios have a human right to welfare before the natural hazard occurred. The people could still claim that right during the disaster and the duty-holders should still be responsible for providing those goods, regardless of the surrounding events. Likewise, the human right to welfare applies to those people affected, before and after a natural hazard occurs, just as it does to all humans. In accordance with the universality of the human right to welfare, the provision of life-saving and life-sustaining assistance during a natural hazard should be given universally to all those affected.

The level of need and the urgency with which welfare needs to be delivered are the only things that change from normal to disaster times. It is the case that natural hazards and the resulting disasters often cause chaos which disrupts the normal flow of basic provisions necessary for life. However, regardless of whether a state is experiencing relative calm or an emergency, the international community is obligated to support all humans with a sub-standard level of welfare (Deng, 2010, p. 255). A mechanism for swift and efficient delivery of the goods and services required for survival is therefore necessary in order to realise this moral obligation.

6.3.3 Intervention in support of welfare in natural hazard scenarios

I argue that intervention is an appropriate mechanism for the swift and efficient delivery of that which is required for survival in natural hazard scenarios. I base this argument first on the fact that intervention is already used as such a mechanism in similar situations where people's lives are threatened. Second, the international community has a duty to intervene to restore the goods that come under the scope of the right to welfare to a population when the population is being deprived of welfare in non-natural hazard situations. Likewise, then, it has the same duty to provide welfare in natural hazard scenarios, with force if necessary.

First, intervention is used as a mechanism for providing the goods associated with the human right to welfare in humanitarian emergencies. In the aftermath of the peacekeeping mission in Kosovo, for example, Tony Blair went to the Commons to ask for additional support for the Kosovan people under threat from Milosevic's dictatorial regime. He argued the intervention was required because of a duty to save lives (Blair, 1999). Additionally, Blair suggested that action on behalf of those humans in the Balkans would maintain peace and security in Europe.

As a result of this speech and diplomatic discussions at the time, the international community organised and launched a peacekeeping mission to the Balkans. It is therefore evident that the international community supports (at least the idea of) upholding human rights in order to create international peace and security.

Similarly, then, the international community should likewise be prepared to intervene to support the scope of the human right to welfare in natural hazard cases because they are ethically comparable. In the Myanmar case, people were dying or at least suffering when assistance could have been provided. Just as Blair made the case that "we must act" in a conflict situation, I make the case that "we must act" to save those suffering a similar fate in the aftermath of a natural hazard.

Furthermore, in conflict situations the rights of the human are already taken into account. If instead of an earthquake, Myanmar faced a conflict situation and people were displaced because of fighting, we would worry that their access to basic goods necessary for survival was hindered and possibly consider, and at least have the mechanism required, for intervention. Then, it is reasonable to suggest that if human welfare (i.e. access to basic life-saving and life-sustaining goods) is a concern in conflict situations it should be an equal concern in natural hazard scenarios. For just as humans are equally deserving of the goods associated with the human right to welfare no matter how it is grounded, humans are equally deserving of assistance no matter the type of emergency they face. So, the type of emergency should have no bearing on whether an intervention commences.

I turn now to discussing the role of force in natural hazard interventions. Since the Convention on the Prevention of Genocide, military intervention has been used to ensure that the human right to welfare is enjoyed by all. The human right to welfare is a positive right in that it requires that the duty-bearer act so as to uphold life and well-being. If a government cannot or will not fulfil that duty, affected humans are owed that duty by the international community, who must discharge it, even if an armed intervention is necessary. The decision to use force does not change the fact that there is a basic minimum owed to humans or that we in the international community have a duty to provide the goods associated with that right to welfare (Shue, 1980).

And so, the human right to welfare is enough in itself to justify intervention. Ignoring basic human needs in the aftermath of a natural hazard denies an affected population the human right to welfare. Furthermore, if intervention is morally acceptable in a conflict situation to uphold the human right to welfare than it is morally required in a natural hazard to uphold the human right to welfare because the morally salient features are comparable in both cases.

6.3.4 Responses to possible criticisms

I conclude this section by discussing two possible objections to my argument. First, if the human right to welfare can ground a case for military intervention it might imply that states ought to intervene militarily to address extreme poverty where the domestic government is not doing enough to alleviate the situation. Second, my argument for natural hazard intervention based on the human right to welfare might justify interventions where the domestic government has not done enough to prepare for a possible natural hazard.

Poverty is a structural issue, the alleviation of which will not be achieved by a one-time intervention by foreign governments. There are actions to be carried out to alleviate poverty before intervention should be considered. Indeed, poverty requires cooperation across countries as well as the implementation of new economic and political policies nationally. Over time, possibly over decades, these changes will alleviate the burdens that contribute to endemic poverty. Following from the need for structural changes over time, poverty, while urgent, does not constitute an emergency situation in the way I am discussing here. It is a slow onset emergency for which interjections of assistance will be helpful but imminent death or lack of all basic welfare are not as urgent as say those in a natural hazard or genocide situation.

As to the issue of under-preparedness, an unprepared government may still effectively respond and work towards restoring the goods associated with a basic level of welfare after a natural hazard. If, however, under-preparation (or not preparing at all) results in a government being unable to provide assistance in the aftermath of a natural hazard then an intervention may be required. Alternatively, if a government has not adequately prepared for a disaster under current international norms, that government is able to ask the international community for help. At a minimum, the national government can consent to the delivery of assistance. If the government rejects assistance *and* they are not able to provide adequate assistance themselves then we are in the same situation as any other country unwilling to provide assistance to its people. In this way, under-preparedness may contribute to the need for an intervention but is not a trigger in itself.

6.4 Conclusion

I began this chapter by explaining how the current laws and standards would play out post-natural hazard. Using this information, in Section 6.2 I outlined problems with adhering to the status quo and what international laws and norms suggest should happen in the aftermath of a natural hazard.

In Section 6.3, I made my case as to why we should intervene in natural hazard scenarios based on the duties associated with the human right to welfare. I explained why the human right to welfare is important and why not intervening in natural hazard scenarios is immoral: it ignores the international community's responsibilities associated with the human right.

From this we are required to uphold the duties associated with the human right to welfare – even during natural hazard scenarios – and intervention is likewise morally required despite any claims that sovereignty should be observed. In the next chapter, I set out the policy necessary for determining when natural hazard intervention is just based on Just War criteria as well as respond to possible objections to my central argument.

Notes

1 The situation in Haiti is discussed in more detail in Section 8.4.1.Additionally, while laws are firm, they are not always interpreted in the same way. The complexity of disaster scenarios and conflict means that each emergency is judged on its own circumstances set against the backdrop of the period of time in which it is occurring.

2 Yet even the principles of neutrality, impartiality and independence may create a normative constraint to the provision of assistance in situations where a national government has not specifically requested or consented to international assis-

tance. The Geneva Conventions of 1949 and Additional Protocol I of 1977 set out the rules associated with assistance to those fighting in, affected by or providing assistance in an armed conflict (ICRC, 1977). Adhering to the principles of neutrality, impartiality and independence requires a would-be intervener to abstain from intervening in conflict situations when consent cannot be garnered. Hence, aid delivered without national consent will, necessarily, bypass a national government.

3 Additionally, see Section 7.2.4 for discussion on how militaries are not perceived as neutral. Assistance in general can be delivered neutrally. The Red Cross, for example, maintains neutrality as one of its fundamental principles (IFRC, 2017). However, the Red Cross seeks consent from the affected country before entering and delivering their service. Consider, however, that an intervention carried out without the consent of the affected country and with the resources of another country may meet with hostility once in country. There will also likely be factions vying for power in the political vacuum that can sometimes occur after large-scale natural hazards. Hence there are situations in which assistance delivered without the consent of an affected government will be considered an invasion of some sort. This means that an intervention may need to have a military component to protect the aid and those assisting as they will be seen as an enemy or similar.

4 This is not always the case in situations in which the government is unable to request assistance as inability to consent does not necessarily imply non-neutrality. There are situations, however, where the international community will be taking sides by delivering assistance and an intervention will not be neutral. I hold that forceful assistance delivery is not neutral as it will be done for an affected group in violation of another group's wishes. The international community will have taken sides and hence will not be neutral.

5 I recognise that the events described here do not qualify as genocide or a wilful violation of human rights law. As a consequence, we cannot commence an international intervention according to the doctrine of RtoP. However, the RtoP doctrine should not be the only mechanism through which humans are saved from disastrous circumstances.

7 Natural hazard intervention policy

Process, conditions, constraints and objections

Thus far I have argued that natural hazard intervention is required in certain situations. Despite the unlikelihood that political will can be rallied or the fact that responding to natural hazards around the world with interventions will be burdensome, natural hazard intervention policy must be created so that what we should do to support other humans has already been fleshed out. Those humans owed assistance may not get it without the creation of such policy. The type of intervention policy I argue for will reaffirm that the human right to welfare requires the international community to intervene in relevant cases. In this chapter, I set out the ethical framework and the moral justification required when countries and international organisations should intervene in response to human welfare issues in the aftermath of a natural hazard. I refer to this framework as *jus ad interventum.*

In 7.1, I explain the importance of preparedness for an ethical delivery of post-emergency assistance as well as what preparedness alone cannot do. I then articulate my policy proposal – jus ad interventum – in Section 7.2 which is based on the six criteria of Just War Theory. I also discuss the possible implications of developing and using my proposal.

With any new policy, especially one dismissed as too difficult, there are obvious conditions and constraints. Section 7.3 is devoted to possible objections to intervention in natural hazard emergencies and my responses. These include imperialism, long-term effects of an intervention, dirty hands, demandingness and the lack of political will. Finally, in Section 7.4, I conclude with a summary of my suggested framework for a military disaster intervention policy in the aftermath of a natural hazard.

7.1 Preparedness

I previously explained the relevance of preparedness to the disaster cycle (preparedness, response, recovery, repeat) and how it helps governments avoid large-scale suffering of humans affected by a natural hazard. There are two aspects of preparedness to consider such that the international community is prepared to intervene should a national government be unable or unwilling to provide for the needs of its people in the aftermath of a natural hazard. First, adequate national preparedness will normally utilise all available domestic capabilities, including how and when international disaster relief should be integrated into a domestic response and should include being prepared to request disaster relief. Second, even the best prepared national governments may still be overwhelmed by events and be unable to consent to assistance. So, in addition to disaster relief preparedness, foreign response bodies should prepare for a possible intervention.

7.1.1 National preparedness and domestic capabilities

Domestic preparedness for natural hazard response includes planning for and putting measures in place before an emergency occurs. For example, reducing water consumption when drought conditions threaten a community or local efforts to create shelter facilities. Domestic preparedness is a necessary (operationally and ethically) step in creating effective disaster response should the need to respond arise. Accordingly, all countries usually develop preparedness plans for natural hazard response.

National response operations are quite often enough to adequately address the needs of those affected. In the event that domestic stock piles and relief capacity are not enough to respond to a specific disaster, disaster relief is available. Disaster relief (Section 3.1.3) (meaning foreign) assistance may be provided with the consent of the affected government by international bodies which have also carried out preparedness measures (stockpiling, search and rescue team exercises, etc.). Foreign resources are still components of a properly prepared domestic disaster response as the supplies and personnel can be integrated upon request.

Additionally, countries have very recently developed plans for the integration of foreign assistance. For example, in the aftermath of Hurricane Katrina, the US Government developed procedures for the integration of foreign assistance into domestic disaster response to account for regulatory and border control issues that will likely occur during a natural hazard response where national responders are overwhelmed (DHS/FEMA, 2015). This plan, however, will only be used when the US government chooses to use it and foreign responders must wait for a request and/or consent from the US government to provide assistance.

Domestic preparedness which includes international support of this sort will necessarily include diplomacy and international coordination with multiple domestic and international agencies and the development of procedures for action (Harper, 2009). If the international community's support is necessary, all efforts should be made to negotiate the delivery of assistance in the aftermath of a natural hazard just as the Emergency Relief Coordinator's policies dictate (Section 3.1.3). So, adequate national preparedness measures will account for operational readiness to respond to natural hazards using domestic and international resources.

7.1.2 Beyond the best laid plans

As evidenced by lessons learned from previous disasters, natural hazard emergency assistance will be provided when a national government requests it or consents to offers made by foreign bodies. However, there is an assumption that a national government will still be in charge of the disaster response. Instead, I argue that international community preparedness must also cover preparedness to respond when a national government is unable to request/consent to assistance. As mentioned in Section 5.1, adequate domestic preparedness may not be enough for appropriate assistance to reach those affected by a natural hazard.

Politicians and laypeople will likely suggest that unsolicited, unwanted and resisted international interventions have produced terrible consequences in the past and will likely cause similar consequences in the future. I address the long-term consequences of the international community preparing for natural hazard intervention in Section 7.3.2. For now, whilst we do not have a system currently (and this may minimise the terrible consequences brought about by intervention), we risk maximizing the number of people left to die in the aftermath of a natural hazard when governments are unable or unwilling to respond. Preparing is appropriate so that we can act on our duty to minimise the further loss of certain goods associated with a minimum level of welfare after a natural hazard.

7.2 A new policy for post-natural hazard intervention

In the previous chapter, I made the case for why intervention is required in some natural hazard scenarios. I now offer a framework for the development of a natural hazard intervention policy, which provides the necessary conditions in which a post-natural hazard intervention would be justified. As with any decision to utilise military force, the international community must decide if certain criteria will be met and if, having met those criteria, an intervention should proceed. In this section, I detail the criteria to be considered ahead of the decision to stage an intervention when a national government is unable or unwilling to support the needs of its people.

To establish the criteria for intervention, I borrow heavily from Just War Theory and adapt its criteria for the operational requirements of natural hazard scenarios. As before, each of the conditions is individually necessary and when all criteria have been met there is sufficient justification for intervention. While the Just War Criteria were developed in part for decision making in going to war, it has also been used as criteria for defending the innocent (Conces, 2001, p. 144). Hence its application to natural hazard scenarios is appropriate as well.

In most natural hazard scenarios, a national government is able to respond to offers of assistance. Acceptance of those offers is usually based on both general need and political will. Regardless of the reason, an acceptance of international assistance implies both willingness and an ability to interact with the international community. In these situations, intervention is unnecessary and inappropriate because a national government is willing and able to respond themselves or integrate external assistance into the domestic response operation. The national government is fulfilling its first-order duties to its people.

However, when a government is unable or unwilling to provide for the needs of its people the duty to provide for the security and political rights of individuals as well as for human welfare still exists. Caney explains that there should be a "back-up" duty-bearer to "fulfil the role that the original duty-bearer should have performed" (Caney, 2013, p. 155). I argued in previous sections that the second-order duty-bearer, namely the international community, has a responsibility to provide for the goods associated with the human right to welfare as well as national and international security. Here, an intervention may be required to support the needs of those affected.[1]

As we saw in the case of Myanmar's Cyclone Nargis, there is no precedent for the international community to act when a government is unwilling to react to a large-impact natural hazard. I argue that in situations like these the duty to respond may require the use of military assets. Assistance delivered in a political vacuum or against the wishes of a national government may be met with an opposing force. Using military personnel will provide safe working environments for aid workers. Additionally, assistance delivered without the official consent of the affected country goes against the norm of non-intervention. It may thus spark violence from the population or violence from remaining officials and members of the military. Accordingly, intervention which acts on second-order duties must be labelled as such – as an intervention – and must adhere to rules associated with an intervention if it is to be considered just.

So, in this section, I provide six conditions which must all be met in order for a natural hazard intervention to be just. It is important to note that these criteria assume the problematic nature of interventions in general and, at the same time, address the ethical issues supporting the interventions in the first place. Meeting these criteria will help to argue against any ethical objections to intervention (Section 6.3). When I argue that there is a requirement to intervene in this chapter I focus mainly on the requirement to intervene to provide the goods associated with the human right to welfare. Human rights have a higher priority than all other types of rights and thus relying on the human right to welfare to justify an intervention policy is the simplest and clearest way to develop the jus ad interventum criteria.

7.2.1 Inability/unwillingness of a government to respond themselves

Currently, the default way of responding to a natural hazard is for a state to take care of its own disaster response. This is for operational reasons as outlined in the Oslo Guidelines. Accordingly, all local, national and international preparedness and diplomatic efforts should be exhausted before considering an intervention lest we undermine ongoing response operations. Intervening without exhausting all domestic capacities and without seeking authorisation from the affected government would also be unjust as it would be an ill-considered interference. Additionally, it may unnecessarily undermine the sovereignty of the given state.

In order to qualify as a just intervention we must ensure that a government is actually unable or unwilling to accept assistance or engage in diplomatic discussions. Let us first consider a scenario in which a government is simply unwilling to accept assistance. The international community can decide if a government is "unwilling" to provide assistance by assessing whether the violation of rights is systemic. Traditionally, decisions to engage in a humanitarian intervention are based on human rights abuses which are state-directed or based on tradition and custom (Conces, 2001, p. 139). If the human rights abuses are state-directed, the government in question is complicit and therefore actively participating in depriving citizens certain rights. When human rights abuse is understood as customary, the offenses are carried out (possibly) by the government but, more importantly, are endemic in society. A coercive intervention, as I defend, would be justified because any unwilling government is, by my definition, carrying out a state-directed plan to avoid international assistance even in violation of the rights of its citizens.

International consensus on whether a government is "unable" to consent to assistance will rely on information gathered at the time. The most straightforward way for the international community to determine this is to decide whether the national government possesses traits of a "failed state": the military, police, civil service, the system of justice and leadership are all failing. A highly functioning state which is demonstrating characteristics of a failed state will qualify as a state unable to respond to the needs of its people. In situations where a country demonstrates characteristics of a failed state *before* the natural hazard, it is likely that an international intervention will be more contentious. If a humanitarian intervention was not carried out before a natural hazard, those arguing for a natural hazard intervention will need to explain how the situation has changed and thus why an intervention is necessary using this system specifically as opposed to that which should have triggered humanitarian intervention. This determination can be made through adherence to the Just War Criteria.

7.2.2 Just cause

I begin the discussion of the just cause criterion with imminent and large-scale threat to life and welfare. I then move to a discussion of killing versus letting die and how we can interpret this to determine if there is a just cause for intervention.

For humanitarian intervention for human rights abuses, the genocide threshold is considered (Conces, 2001; United Nations, 1948). This threshold does not provide a specific number of people that need to die before an intervention is deemed to have a just cause. Rather, the genocide threshold is a carefully weighed condition in which "a substantial part" of a population is targeted for annihilation, motivated by race, ethnicity or hegemonic desires (The United States Holocaust Memorial Museum, n.d.). The just cause condition for humanitarian interventions is satisfied if a population is targeted in this way.

Both proponents and opponents of intervention will likely find an unquantifiable threshold for determining just cause to be problematic. For proponents of intervention, a certain threshold may be too high thus allowing too many people to die before action is taken. For opponents of intervention, the unquantifiable nature of the genocide threshold raises concerns that intervention will come too often. Even those countries that agree that natural hazard intervention should occur will have to deal with more frequent requests for intervention. Thus the genocide threshold may leave too much open to circumstances and require action from unwilling parties. This debate is not new, though, and will be addressed in Section 7.3.4.

The concept of genocide thresholds provides a useful analogue for death as an outcome of natural hazard. The genocide threshold sets a precedent for not quantifying the number of affected people required before there is a just cause for intervention. I argue using the same logic: deprivation of basic goods in the aftermath of a natural hazard is a human rights abuse which results in large-scale harm. It deprives peoples of, at a minimum, a dignified life and at worst, their actual lives. As I argued in Chapter 4, mass risk of death, mass homelessness, lack of access to clean water and malnutrition are enough to qualify as failures to respect the human right to welfare.

So, instead of invoking the genocide threshold in my list of criteria for just intervention, I argue that imminent threat to life and welfare on a mass scale likewise qualifies as a just cause for intervention. The just cause for intervention in genocide scenarios is the imminent threat to human life on a massive scale. The cause of death during a genocide or humanitarian emergency – firing squad, gas chamber or lack of food – should, however, be irrelevant; all represent large-scale suffering which threatens full enjoyment of the human right to welfare.[2] This means that the large-scale threat to human life caused by deprivation of the goods associated with the human right to basic welfare is equally a just cause for intervention in relevant natural hazard scenarios based on a violation of the human right to welfare.

Some will likely criticise my assumption that refusal of natural hazard assistance is a rights violation equal to that of genocide and contend that there is something worse about genocide. Those critics can object to the equal badness of these deaths in two ways. One way is to argue that in genocide situations it is not the threat to human life that is the just cause for intervention. Instead, it is the harm the government causes by *killing* so many people. A government which refuses to help its citizens in the aftermath of a natural hazard is not *killing* its people and so we cannot really compare the harms. Genocide is objectively worse.

The second way of objecting to my claim that refusal of assistance post-natural hazard and genocide may be equally bad is to argue that in natural hazard situations a national government is *allowing* people to die rather than killing. Allowing could then be argued to be not as bad a harm as killing. So, when a national government *allows* its people to die, the harm is not equal to that incurred by genocide. As a result, there is no just cause for intervention in natural hazard scenarios when a government is unwilling to provide assistance.[3]

I have three responses to these objections. In establishing these responses, I first set out the distinction between killing and letting die, then show how creating a barrier to aid is at least as bad as letting people die, and finally demonstrate how the creation of barriers to aid to argue that the intention of an unwilling government – whether killing or creating a barrier – has the same purpose and thus are equally as bad for those affected. In this way, I will argue that killing by means of genocide and creating a barrier to aid post-natural hazard are equal harms that establish the same just cause for intervention.

I start from a generally held position that there is a moral distinction between the harm involved in genocide (the killing of humans) and the mass threat to human life. There is a doing (killing) vs allowing (letting die) distinction which can be applied in the natural hazard and genocide equivalence debate (Woollard, 2012). For Philippa Foot, the moral distinction between killing and letting die is a matter of sequence: if my agency triggered a sequence of events then I am morally accountable for any harm caused (Woollard, 2012, pp. 449–450; Foot, 2002). So, if I push a rock off of a cliff and it kills someone below, I have *killed* by triggering a sequence of events (the push, the fall, the landing) that resulted in someone's death.

Conversely, a natural hazard is not triggered by human agency.[4] Using that logic, the sequence of events that resulted in certain people's deaths cannot be understood as *killing*. Instead, any actions which deprive a person of necessary welfare goods in this situation is simply allowing death. Thus, because a natural hazard was not triggered by human agency those people responding or not responding cannot be said to be *killing* – they did not trigger the sequence of events. A government here would simply be letting its people die.

Alternatively, Hasner's interpretation of the doing vs allowing debate offers evidence that removal of a barrier is an act of doing a certain kind of harm (1999). Removing a rock that would have stopped a person falling all the way to the bottom is still an action. Thus for Hasner removing a patient's life support machine is *doing* a harm. If applied to natural hazard response scenarios, removing basic goods available before the hazard may similarly be seen as 'doing' harm, even if it is not killing per se.

There may be disagreement on what counts as doing and what counts as allowing. However, there is general agreement that allowing is a lesser harm than doing. Accordingly, it can be argued that allowing people to die in situations where death is imminent is not as bad as the active killing in genocide situations. Whilst this may be true, letting a large number of people die is still harmful. I therefore argue that killing and letting die on the scale in question is still harmful and represent equally just causes for intervention.

There is also a second response to the objections stated previously. Specifically, a government unwilling to assist its people or consent to assistance may indeed not be killing. However, they are creating a barrier to assistance which is a harm that is perhaps at least almost equal to that of killing.

Hasner suggests that there is a third type of harm in addition to doing and allowing which he labels "preventing people from being saved" (1999).[5] He argues that preventing assistance from reaching those in need is an act of allowing harm only. Similar to Foot's discussion of a sequence of events qualifying the type of harm, Hasner explains that preventing someone from having their life saved depends on a sequence of events, a reasonable understanding of possible outcomes, and motives behind any such actions that figure into an agent's actions. He therefore argues that preventing someone from obtaining the benefit of having their life saved is a distinctly different type of harm.

That being said, both types of harm are what he calls *lethal* harms in that they end in death. In this way, both are morally objectionable to the same degree because they result in a particular death (Hasner, 1999, pp. 284–285). So, because both genocide and the prevention of having one's life saved in the aftermath of a natural hazard are lethal harms resulting in death they are prima facie objectionable and can be considered moral equivalents (Hasner, 1999).[6]

I am not arguing for intervention on the grounds of human rights abuses or genocide in this chapter. Rather, I am arguing that the crimes being committed are similar and thus the responsibility of the international community to respond is likewise similar to that of other large-scale human rights abuses or genocide. Deprivation of basic welfare in the aftermath thus exists as a just cause for intervention because it is a lethal harm.[7]

Here, I have explained that relevant information at the time will be considered at the time of the natural hazard to determine whether there is a just cause for intervention. Discussions amongst international officials will use this information to decide whether the type and extent of the threat to welfare (whether it is a lethal harm) that exists constitutes a just cause for intervention. As I have explained, whether a government has purposefully killed or simply allowed its people to die is irrelevant when determining if there is a just cause for intervention. Even without a precise set death threshold, we must at least hold that at some point mass death in the aftermath of a natural hazard requires and is a just cause for an intervention. This is not the current norm.

7.2.3 Proportionality

According to the principles of the Just War Theory, proportionality establishes the quantifiable restrictions on an intervention – how many resources to assign to the operation, how long the interveners should remain in the country and so forth. Proportionality is best understood in terms of whether in obtaining some object *x*, the good outweighs the bad. The "relevant good" of a natural hazard intervention would be the enjoyment of the human right to welfare, the avoidance of suffering and death (Dobos, 2012, pp. 49–50).

The possible burdens include the detrimental long-term effects of an intervention (i.e. dependence on foreign aid). There is also the effect an intervention will have on the lives of the interveners themselves as well as the socio-economic impact an intervention will have on the domestic population of the intervening country. All of these issues should be weighed to determine if intervening is a proportional response.

Furthermore, proportionality requires that we adjust the means to the ends desired (Walzer, 2006, pp. 119–120). If the goal of an intervention is to bring about a stable peace post-conflict, we must ensure that the way we go about this will result in just that. Consider, once again, the example of the 2003 US invasion of Afghanistan discussed in Section 3.2.2 as an example. The United States aims at international peace and security but may need to adjust the means of achieving that end in order to satisfy proportionality.

Let us consider what a disproportionate natural hazard intervention would be like. Consider a thunderstorm which creates localised flooding and damaged basements in the affected area. This natural hazard does not require foreign military intervention, regardless of whether a national government is helping those affected. To send military forces in response to such a storm would be completely disproportionate to the needs of those affected. This would be an unjust intervention because an intervention is not required operationally to re-establish the area and would not benefit those affected. A small-scale natural hazard as the one described does not demonstrate a purposeful and consistent abuse of human rights even if people have died because of the storm or the subsequent floods. Storms, like all natural hazards, have the capacity to destroy lives and livelihoods but this does not mean that an intervention would be a proportionate, and thus just, response.

Furthermore, an intervention would be unjust in this small-scale natural hazard situation because it would overwhelm national capacities. A foreign military presence in a small area coping with a small emergency will likely take supplies away from those affected, hinder a community's ability to re-establish itself, and undermine people's ability to recover post-disaster. National responders, even with the best preparedness possible, may not be able to support every person affected but this does not mean that an intervention is required as the good being provided would not outweigh the bad created.

Proportionality is a necessary criterion for deciding whether to intervene in a natural hazard scenario. A proportionate response will be carried out in response to an abuse of the human right to welfare where the possible benefits of doing so outweigh the possible negatives. Proportionality does not allow for an intervention in small-scale emergencies in which a severe risk to a population's life does not exist.

7.2.4 Last resort[8]

A military intervention for the purpose of delivering assistance post-natural hazard should always be a last resort. Force is a mechanism of politics to be used when all other mechanisms have failed (Çlausewitz, 1997). Likewise, military intervention in natural hazard scenarios is so drastic a measure that it should be used only when there is absolutely no other way to restore those goods associated with the human right to welfare to those who have lost them.

Before resorting to military operations we should explore how best to make an offer of assistance. Offers can be made officially or unofficially depending on how the offer will be perceived by the officials of the country affected. Official offers can be made from one government to another government or from an international body to a government. In some cases political hostilities may make a government to government offer seem patronizing or imperialistic. International bodies may have less political baggage and hence be a better negotiator. Likewise, an unwilling government may fear political backlash. Alternatively, assistance can be offered through back channels and in coordination with political dealings. All of these options for delivery of assistance should be explored before resorting to military operations.

When the point of intervention is to support the lives and livelihoods of those whose human right to welfare is not being respected, the go-to answer cannot be to risk the lives of those intervening. Nor can the use of military force, possibly against the very civilians it is intent on protecting, be the first solution to the failings of a national government. Such an intervention would be an unjust use of force. When weighed against all other possible ways of supporting the human right to welfare, a military intervention must therefore only be considered when all other non-lethal forms of intervention have been exhausted.

With this in mind, we should not shy away from using force when it is necessary. Force should instead be used in conjunction with disaster assistance for two reasons. First, if the government was originally unwilling to accept assistance there is a risk that they may use force against the relief workers tied to the intervention. Those intervening need protection from an assault for themselves and the assistance. Second, if the intervention is being done in a country unable to provide consent for assistance, there is a significant possibility that armed groups or militias will have seized control in areas. Interveners present in a natural hazard situation, and there on behalf of the people affected, must be afforded every opportunity to protect themselves. By not recognizing that the use of force may be necessary, we are putting our responders in danger.

This does not necessarily mean that force should be used against the national government. Armed bands or simply desperate people may also fire on aid workers. Restrictions on the use of force similar to the restrictions placed on peacekeeping forces should of course apply. UN peacekeepers are ordered only to use force in self-defence; the use of force is meant as protection for interveners and as a shield for the assistance being delivered (United Nations, 2015). Likewise, the use of force in a natural hazard intervention should only be used in self-defence.

Furthermore, last resort as a criterion for a just intervention helps to ensure that the use of force as an option has been thoroughly scrutinised and debated amongst members of the international community. This process of determining whether the use of force is necessary will allow the other just war principles to be explored. The delivery of assistance will then necessarily constitute a just intervention in line with proportionality, just cause and right intention.

In sum, military intervention should be a mechanism of last resort for the delivery of those objects of the human right to welfare necessary for survival. When considering the use of force, policy makers need to recognise that the assistance will no longer be seen as neutral and that some responders' lives may be lost. For this reason, we should never entertain this option until it is the only option left.

7.2.5 Right authority

When deciding whether to exercise the use of force, policymakers must meet the right authority requirement. Not all of those with the capacity to respond have the authority to respond. Corporations, NGOs and private citizens may all have the financial capacity, the know-how, or even the right intentions to make for a properly exercised intervention. However, in order to stop rogue actors and maintain legitimate responsibility, international norms restrict the use of force to official government bodies.

More broadly, the use of force is a central tenet of the state system and an authority only bestowed upon states and the international community as a coordinated mechanism of states.[9] Accordingly, implementation of Chapter VII of the UN Charter (which allows for international action) requires international consensus. Likewise, then, determining whether an intervention has the right authority will flow from appropriate bodies and from international consensus. Right authority has two complimentary components: right authority to decide to intervene and to intervene.

There are both legal and moral aspects of the authority to decide. First, who has the legal authority, mandated by the international community, to decide when an intervention is justified? Any unilateral decision to intervene into the affairs of another state is to be discouraged in all scenarios.[10] The UN Security Council, for example, has the authority to authorise an intervention and override sovereignty when the members have come to a collective decision (Fixdal & Smith, 1998, p. 292). Once again, this authority was established by international consensus when the UN Charter was originally established.

Unilateral intervention is arguably likely to be seen as an imperialist intervention without the legitimate authority of the international community. With more stakeholders involved in the decision making there will be more people responsible for the intervention. With this a proper system of checks and balances on the power of states is maintained.

In addition to a legal *right authority* to intervene, let us also consider who has the appropriate moral authority to decide that an intervention should occur. For an intervention to be ethical it must be authorised multilaterally. As Walzer suggests, multilateral authorisation lends moral legitimacy to an intervention as it will minimise the imperialist or selfish tendencies of individual states (1995, p. 63, 2002). A cosmopolitan approach to intervention would also support the need for multilateral authorisation. Archibugi suggests that an intervention should be decided by those without coercive power. He continues that an intervention should be carried out by those who may lose more from intervening than those on whose behalf the intervention was carried out: by a "UN institution" and under the "UN flag" (2004). This will provide moral legitimacy to the intervention because the authority stems from institutionalised norms of cosmopolitan justice pertaining to right authority. Additionally, being held accountable to one's peers will ensure that motivations are checked. The intervention can be decided based on moral, as opposed to simply political or economic, justifications. Thus the decision to elevate an operation from disaster relief to intervention should be made collectively by the international community.

Indeed, selfish intentions of individual states will likely exist at the forefront of negotiations. Slowly, however, Walzer argues that the needs of humanity (i.e. the moral reasons for intervention or rather the *just cause* for intervening) will be one among many reasons for intervening (2002). Through multilateral negotiation, the needs of humanity will rise to the top of the list of reasons for intervention. These needs can then be acted upon through an intervention. The mission will have been developed with the authority of the international community.

While the decision to intervene must be multilateral, the intervention itself need not be (though it can be) multilateral in order for the intervention to be considered to have the right authority. The institution that should deploy is the institution that can deploy quickest and with the authority of the international community.

Similar to decisions about who has the authority to decide to intervene, there are legal and moral components to the *right authority* criterion for intervention. Legally, only official national and international governmental bodies may do the actual intervening. Under the state system, force may only be exercised by official bodies. Private military and security bodies do not have international authority to intervene. Likewise a national authority should not be delegated to a private body to act out an intervention.

The current international authority for response deployments post-natural hazard is the Office for the Coordination of Humanitarian Affairs (OCHA) and the Emergency Relief Coordinator (ERC). As explained elsewhere, the ERC's role is to coordinate the assistance offered and consented to by a country affected by a disaster triggered by a natural hazard. OCHA and the ERC would thus be an appropriate choice as the body with the legal right authority to intervene.

Now, OCHA and the ERC operate as they do because they hold the collective will from those legally and morally allowed to use force.[11] With this in mind, the right authority for carrying out an intervention may continue to be the ERC if it is able to liaise with either the Security Council or UN General Assembly in such a way as to gain authority and act quickly and efficiently. Accordingly, any actions taken by the Coordinator's office will have the full weight of the UN behind it.[12]

Multilateral consensus will hopefully bestow some level of moral legitimacy on the intervention. That said, there are several practical reasons for seeking multilateral consensus. First, if a government makes the decision to intervene with others as opposed to on its own and it is the "wrong" decision, there is at least some legitimacy to the decision and justified procedures would have been followed. Also, unjust interventions may trigger other unjust interventions. When one country acts without authority it undermines the authority of the international society of states. If approval and/or admonishment are not distributed for unauthorised interventions, there is little incentive for states to seek approval from the international community in the future.

And so, right authority is a necessary criterion for an intervention to be considered just. The decision to intervene must be made by those with the right authority, namely a multilateral body. Once the decision to intervene has been made, a (governmental) unilateral or multilateral operation may act, as long as the political will to carry out the multilateral authorisation is present.

7.2.6 Right intention

Once we know who or what has the right authority, we can explore the intentions of those right authorities. Right intentions are those reasons which justify the military action and are not given simply as "cover for the pursuit of other aims" (McMahan, 2006, p. 5). Hence, in order for an intervention to be just the authorities must have a right intention.

Analysis of the invasion of Iraq in 2012 suggests that the originally offered justification for the invasion had to do with preventing the spread and use of chemical and biological weapons (Wallechinsky, 2011). By invading, the United States asserted that it was stopping imminent terrorist attacks. The United States also claimed to be attempting to prevent the spread and use of chemical and biological weapons by terrorists (Wallechinsky, 2011). If this was the entire reason then there clearly was a *right intention* to the US invasion of Iraq: preservation of international peace and security is internationally recognised as a reason for going to war.

In the years following, it has become increasingly clear that preventing terrorism did not match the actual intentions of the US government. Various reasons have been claimed: to spread democracy, war profiteering and/or the protection of vital strategic interests (Wallechinsky, 2011). These are not justified "right intentions" for invasion (or, for the purpose of this analysis, intervention). In line with the just cause requirement of Just War Theory, those intervening must be working to prevent human rights abuses and/or restore international peace and security. Preventing the spread of weapons was actually the "cover" for spreading democracy, amongst other things. And so, the US invasion of Iraq did not have a "right intention".

Intervention in the event of a natural hazard must likewise be carried out with a right intention. It must be done to support human rights and/or to ensure international peace and security. As I argue, an intervention when a government is unable or unwilling to provide for the basic needs of its people in the aftermath of a natural hazard is justified if that intervention intends to provide the goods associated with the human right to welfare.

Dobos addresses the possibility of ulterior motives in humanitarian interventions. He explains that all of the intentions associated with an intervention need not be selfless; self-interest can be part of the reason for a state to intervene into another state (Dobos, 2012, p. 66). However, a right intention must exist amongst the justifications offered for intervention in order to satisfy this necessary just war condition.

7.2.7 Long-term consequences

Finally, before a natural hazard intervention commences, decision makers must weigh the possible long-term consequences. Decision makers must also decide if, in line with the requirement of proportionality, the benefits will outweigh the costs. Long-term consequences include the possible impact on those receiving and those providing assistance. An intervention carried out without a big picture view or an exit strategy does not have the needs of those it aims to help in mind. Only when any negative long-term implications of an intervention have been mitigated can the other just criterion be satisfied. Long-term implications fall into three categories (usually). These include the consequences on the individual, regional stability and the international community in general.[13]

First, any intervention should be done to provide for the welfare of individuals affected. I have argued, with others, that the rights of the individual supersede that of the state (Fixdal & Smith, 1998, p. 294). Indeed, individual (human) rights are of the highest priority and hence any intervention must benefit individuals in the long run.

Consider the long-term implications of disaster relief. Shelter is a basic good which is often delivered as part of an earthquake relief. In April 2009, a 6.3 magnitude earthquake hit the town of L'Aquila in central Italy (Squires, 2009). The L'Aquila earthquake destroyed public buildings and homes forcing people into tents to avoid being killed in aftershocks. The tents were well received at first. However, anxiety mounted as the rains made tent-life an unbearable reality as months continued to pass with no suggestion of moving into permanent accommodation (Squires, 2009). The responders did not review the capacity of these facilities in the long term. Hence, decision makers did not adequately determine the long-term implications of the assistance being provided. Accordingly, while the goods associated with basic welfare were delivered, they were not adequately appropriate for long-term displacement.

Second, there are relevant long-term consequences at the regional level. Perpetuating state power and regional dynamics which maintain stability cannot be done at the expense of human welfare (Fixdal & Smith, 1998, p. 294). For example, it is unjust to intervene in order to remove a dictator from power. While an intervention may bolster the welfare of those affected by a natural hazard in that dictatorship, those suffering are used as pawns in a regional vie for power.

Furthermore, if the international community intervenes to save, say, North Koreans from the effects of an earthquake, the interveners risk the wrath of China who will likely see themselves as the regional hegemon. South Koreans may, as a result, be dragged into a regional war. Thus a long-term implication of intervention to support the human right to welfare may be regional imbalance.

Decision makers must likewise consider the effect non-intervention would have on those outside the affected country. Individuals and governments in neighbouring countries will likely have to deal with the aftermath of disaster as well as disease, famine, refugees and possible political unrest. The long-term consequence of non-intervention is likely to be as bad or worse than an intervention which will aim to reduce the levels of death and migration possible in the aftermath of a non-supported natural hazard.

This leads to the final category of long-term implications: global political and economic stability. For example, in the aftermath of the Sri Lankan tsunami, thousands of kilos of rice were donated to the country. While this rice was intended to stop the suffering of those affected it was not useful (BBC Sinhala,

2005). That much rice would likely flood the local market making it impossible for local farmers to sell their rice.

Those offering assistance did not consider global political and economic stability and results were disastrous. Instead of providing assistance in this way, we must develop policy that takes the needs of every human (possibly) affected into consideration. The long-term consequence of destabilizing a region must indeed be considered when deciding whether an intervention would be just. Furthermore, an intervention's ability to maintain some modicum of stability for the region must also be considered.

7.2.8 Summary of just intervention criteria

The criteria I have discussed in this chapter are as follows: inability or unwillingness for a government to respond; just cause; proportionality; last resort; right authority; right intention; long-term consequences. Each is a necessary condition for an intervention to be just. Together, these seven criteria establish a sufficient ethical framework for policy makers to engage in a just intervention. Establishment and use of jus ad interventum criteria is the ethical way forward for post-natural hazard intervention policy.

Like the necessary and sufficient conditions of jus ad bellum, these seven criteria are only useful in determining whether an intervention itself will be just. The guidance I have set out here does nothing to help create jus in bello or just conditions during an intervention. That requires a separate study. And so, to continue my analysis of jus ad interventum (or justice in intervening), I next address possible objections to the development of such an assistance policy in the event of a natural hazard where a government is unable or unwilling to provide the necessary assistance to affected individuals.

7.3 Objections to a post-natural hazard intervention policy

I first discuss the objection that an intervention is really concealing imperialistic tendencies of wealthier and stronger countries. In 7.3.2, I discuss the long-term implications of an intervention: what an intervention means for the interveners and those affected by the disaster. In 7.3.3, I discuss the problem of "dirty hands". In 7.3.4, I review the objection based on the demandingness of creating yet another reason for the international community to intervene. In 7.3.5, I respond to the objection that there is a lack of political will for intervention of this kind and therefore developing a policy is unnecessary.

7.3.1 An intervention conceals imperialist tendencies

Developing countries reasonably worry that an intervener or foreign powers supporting response operations will conceal imperialist tendencies. Indeed, militaries are often seen as a threat simply because they carry weapons (Wiharta et al., 2005, p. 82). An affected country may worry that they will end up a puppet government, beholden to those that "rescued" them from a miserable fate. It could thus be argued that development of a post-natural hazard intervention policy at the global level will make it possible for hegemonic state(s) to "claim exemption from rules it expects other countries to observe" (Nardin, 2005, p. 26).

Sadly, greed and power often drive decisions to support affected communities just as much as do humanitarian considerations. The imperialistic intentions of those offering help are in many cases real and they must be guarded against, particularly when there is a "stronger" and "weaker" power interacting. One need only remember the Afghan people feeling like "sacrificial lambs" after the US-led invasion; permanent war allows for American influence in the country and an ongoing military presence (Faiez & Sraziuso, 2014).

Even if we accept that imperialistic tendencies are a real possibility, we need not accept that the possibility of imperialism is always a reason *not* to intervene. Indeed, there are two ways to respond to this objection. First, international policies already restrict imperialist tendencies of intervening states. By establishing a policy for natural hazard intervention, we have a better chance of keeping imperialist powers in check. Second, an intervention policy which allows for foreign assistance without consent can risk imperialist invasions just as easily as is inviting foreign forces to support a domestically run operation. I will consider these responses in turn.

First, while we cannot prevent hegemons from trying to obtain larger spheres of influence, we can make it more difficult to do so. Humanitarian intervention, properly understood, is grounded in supporting those affected by an atrocity and under the authority of international law (Nardin, 2005, p. 25). Furthermore, the use of force is restricted under international law. Article 2(4) of the charter specifies that the use of force is not to be used in any manner "inconsistent with the Purposes of the United Nations" (United Nations, 2015). Hence, humanitarian intervention is not explicitly allowed for (but it is not prohibited either) (Stanulova, 2010, p. 6). Furthermore, the IFRC promote and utilise the *Guidelines for the Domestic Facilitation and Regulation of International Disaster Relief and Initial Recovery Assistance (IDRL Guidelines)* in their disaster relief programmes. These and other international policies aim to restrict how and when force may be used for humanitarian purposes.

Indeed, aspects of UN Peacekeeping are allowed under Chapters VI, VII, and VIII. However, even here use of force is meant as a tool of "self-defence and [in] defence of the mandate" (United Nations, 2015). Hence, international doctrines provide a mechanism for intervening and set out the possible implications for the intervener if there is an unauthorised use of force. These rules thus support response operations tried, tested and approved by the international community. The rules also ensure that there is a mechanism for admonishing those who do not follow the rules. Accordingly, policies can keep imperialist states in check.

If we look at natural hazard scenarios specifically there are no mechanisms for or means of admonition by the international community in the event of an intervention. In 2007, the United Nation's International Law Commission began the process of developing a multilateral framework on *Protection of Persons in Event of Disasters* (Tokunaga, 2014, pp. 46–53). This framework did nothing to enforce the duty of the international community to respond in the event of a large-scale natural hazard. The requirement of consent and respect for state sovereignty and the state duty to be responsible for its own people remain the guidance for those considering such intervention.

The consistency of the norm of non-intervention for natural hazard response suggests that members of the international community are likely to avoid intervention. However, the consent requirement and resultant non-intervention guidance are clearly not in line with the ethical argument being made herein. I have therefore suggested that a transparent policy for natural hazard intervention is necessary. Transparency, I hope, should calm the fears of those who see intervention as concealment for imperialist tendencies and trigger a normative shift away from non-intervention. Checks and balances to prevent imperialist tendencies of intervening states are built into the structure of my policy proposal.

Having rules in place for humanitarian intervention and peacekeeping operations may therefore provide a better opportunity to keep imperialist powers in check. It is reasonable to expect that natural hazard emergency response will benefit in the same way. At the same time, it is naïve and short-sighted of international policy to maintain a norm of non-intervention because it assumes that no country ever will intervene. If negotiation with the Burmese generals had not gone the way it did after Cyclone Nargis, there is a huge possibility that the international community would have forcibly intervened. We would have had no way of checking imperialist tendencies of interveners in that situation. Therefore, only through the development of an intervention policy now can we even attempt to manage tendencies later.

Second, some give weight to national consent as a pivotal requirement for foreign parties entering and supporting a natural hazard response in order to insulate affected countries from imperialistic threats. Governments hold that the consent requirement ensures that assistance can be integrated into domestic operations. It further ensures that a national government can take the lead in delivering required aid.[14] However, even countries which have granted access to foreign countries are at risk of losing control over self-governance. Consenting to assistance will not always prevent imperialistic intentions.

It could be claimed that creating an intervention policy for natural hazards will remove governmental consent to assistance and therefore blatantly opens the door to imperialist invaders. However, the international community already finds ways around consent if the interveners have the political will and the intention to intervene. Take airdrops as an example. When conflict prevents overland access to people starving, airdrops can supply thousands with food and supplies (IRIN News, 2009). Airdrops are much more expensive than traditional methods of supply delivery and they require skill for accurate drops. That said, if the need is great and the political will is there, those providing disaster relief will find a way to get supplies to those in need.

So, consent ensures that those best placed operationally to deliver assistance are given the space to do so. It keeps leadership in the hands of those with local knowledge and with the interests of their own domestic population at heart. Suggestions that interventions may hide imperialist intentions are justified: imperialist tendencies or intentions will exist regardless of the type of international action under negotiation. Policies which provide checks and balances against imperialist tendencies are put in place so as to prevent rampant and unmitigated imperialism from occurring when a population is at its most vulnerable. A natural hazard intervention policy will provide such a check and is thereby necessary.

7.3.2 Detrimental long-term effects of an intervention

John Holmes, former UN Under-Secretary General for Humanitarian Affairs, has argued that "invading" a country affected by a natural hazard would do nothing to speed the flow of assistance to those without food, shelter and security (Bowley & Erlanger, 2008). All intervention will do is add additional problems to an already destabilised region. People may be assisted in the short term; however, in the long term, the country will have to deal with the political and economic impact of foreign interference.

From this, we can identify three concerns regarding long-term effects of an intervention. First, foreign assistance will likely exacerbate already unstable countries and regions. In this way, interventions may actually bring greater harm to those affected by a natural hazard then if left unaided. Second, international responders are unlikely to stay in-country long enough to bring assistance projects to their necessary ends. Third, foreign assistance workers do not have the same duties to those affected as workers within the same country have.

I begin with the harm caused specifically by an intervention. Interventions are often disastrous, leaving more chaos and bloodshed than would have occurred had the international community left the domestic government to its own devices. For example, in post-US invasion Iraq and the more recent Syrian crisis, it can be argued that unsolicited, unwanted and resisted international interventions have produced terrible consequences: political instability, economic frailty, overdependence on the international system and so forth.

Disaster fatigue is a real phenomenon in which the greater the devastation and the more frequent the devastating events, the less people care about the disaster (Tolin, 2008). Statistics point to the idea that the Myanmar cyclone (2008) and the China earthquake of 2008 received less foreign charity than would have been expected given the size of the disaster. One reason for this is the overwhelming number of disasters which occurred in succession (Associated Press, 2008). And so, it is to be expected that populations and would-be interveners would likely become weary of providing assistance and may therefore cease providing long-term aid.

Furthermore, some argue that change must come from within and therefore any political, economic or operational change must be initiated by those actually affected in order for a long-term integration of change (Walzer,

2002, p. 2). Under the terms of the social contract argued for by Hobbes and Locke, the state has a duty to support the needs of its own citizens. Likewise, we have special duties to compatriots. Hence, duties and obligations are owed to others within the same state and any actions taken on behalf of those affected must also come from within the state if long-term relief activities are to improve the society in question (Dobos, 2012, pp. 123–128). National responders will always know the political, economic and social landscape and be able to provide assistance in line with the long-term, collective goals of the affected community. This point offers us reason to avoid intervention: those affected by a natural hazard will be better off in the long term without the help of foreign sources.

However, these are not arguments for non-intervention. It is true that we cannot guarantee that the outcome of any use of force will be positive; equally we cannot rule out the use of force in general. In line with just war conditions, the long-term effects of an intervention must be considered when weighing whether or not intervention is appropriate (see Section 7.2.7). Following a set of criteria such as those for a Just War (and additionally those criteria established by the Responsibility to Protect) will help to minimise the damage caused by the use of force as that is what the criteria were originally intended to do. Additionally, force will be used proportionately to the needs of the disaster.

I agree with much of the argument regarding detrimental long-term effects of an intervention. There are many situations in which an intervention would have created further problems for an effected state (i.e. an intervention into the United States in the aftermath of Hurricane Katrina). However, intervention must be established as a tool of the international community so that it can support the welfare of affected individuals – even if it is not used frequently. Sierra Leone (1999–2005) and Burundi (2004–2006) are both seen as successful international peacekeeping operations which benefited the lives of those affected by the conflict (Henderson, 2015; Reuters, 2008; United Nations, 2006).

As these and other peacekeeping operations remind us, there are definite concerns about the long-term effects of an intervention. However, there are situations in which intervening is not a means to detrimental ends. Indeed, sometimes, intervention will save lives and provide for the welfare of those affected by an emergency when a national government is unable or unwilling to provide safety.

7.3.3 Dirty hands

The third objection often raised in response to the idea of military interventions for good causes is that of "dirty hands". "Dirty hands" dilemmas are those in which it is not possible to achieve a morally good outcome, saving the life of an innocent for example, or fulfil a moral duty, without simultaneously causing some other harmful or morally bad outcome to occur. Thus, in such situations, it is not possible to achieve purely good outcomes. The dirty hands dilemma involves issues of blameworthiness in both ethical and political dilemmas (Sartre, 1948; Robinson, 2007; Walzer, 2004; Gaus, 2003; deWijze, 2013).

In this section I first give a detailed explanation of the dirty hands phenomenon in general and then in intervention scenarios specifically. I also consider the placement of blame on dirty hands actors. I then argue that despite the persistence of dirty hands scenarios and the possibility of blameworthy deeds in natural hazard interventions, intervention is morally required in the type of natural hazard scenarios I discuss.

With my brief definition of dirty hands in mind, consider the following: shooting one man to save the lives of four other men could be thought to be justified at least in certain circumstances (war being the most obvious example). However, while this action may be justified, it would still be considered morally wrong by many. Hence the paradox of dirty hands is this: how can one need to do wrong in order to do what is ethically correct (deWijze, 2013; Gaus, 2003; Williams, 1991, pp. 100–107)?

A natural hazard intervention as I propose may also qualify as a dirty hands situation. If an intervention has satisfied the Just War Criteria outlined previously in this chapter, it can be understood as a just intervention. I argued in Chapter 4 that a natural hazard intervention is in some situations morally required in order to re-establish a basic minimum level of welfare to those who are not being helped by their national government. An intervention can thus be said to be obligatory. However, any use of military force may involve killing or other loss of life and thereby could also be thought to be morally wrong (a dirty hands situation).

Hence because a natural hazard intervention may result in some killing we can say that a natural hazard intervention may result in dirty hands. It follows, then, that if killing occurs, a moral wrong has also occurred and blame will be attributed. So, in explaining how natural hazard interventions may require killing I am assuming that there will be some level of blame aimed at the interveners. Natural hazard interveners will, by extension, have dirty hands. However, as I explain in this section, these interventions are a case of less bad and therefore less blame.

Natural hazard interventions are morally permissible despite the possibility of dirty hands. I begin with a discussion of blame, applying different principles of blame to the natural hazard intervention scenarios argued for in this analysis. From this I make the case that the possibility of dirty hands should not prevent the development of natural hazard intervention policy.

I begin with blame. Michael Otsuka first engages with Principle of Alternate Possibilities (PAP). According to PAP if an action could have been avoided, but wasn't, the actor can be blamed for the outcome of the action (Otsuka, 1998). For example, John pushes Mala down the stairs. We blame John because he did not have to push Mala down the stairs. There were alternate possibilities.

Otsuka offers instead The Principle of Avoidable Blame (PAB). This principle states that one cannot be blamed for carrying out an act if all other options would have deserved more blame (Otsuka, 1998). Using the same example as above, imagine that Mala is going to drop the box she is carrying onto a child sitting on the floor. In attempting to stop the harm occurring to the child, John can push Mala out of the way and down the stairs. According to PAB, John cannot be blamed for pushing Mala down the stairs in this case because, had he chosen any other alternative, he would have been more blameworthy. The PAB is situation-specific, and all options must be weighed at the time that a decision is being made to determine if there are any options available that would be less blameworthy than others. Importantly, according to PAB, even non-action is still a choice that may lead to blameworthy outcomes if an alternative action exists.[15]

The Principle of Avoidable Blame can also be applied to natural hazard intervention scenarios. This provides two options to the international community when a national government is unable or unwilling to aid its own people. Option A is to not intervene militarily and continue to offer relief. The outcome of this option is that people will continue to suffer and die from disaster-related harms when their government is unable or unwilling to assist. Option B involves a military intervention. The international community will save those people affected by the natural hazard but may have to kill people (those preventing aid delivery) in order to deliver that assistance. By applying PAB it is reasonable to carry on with Option B. This is because in carrying out natural hazard interventions according to the Just War Criteria as I detailed, all possible alternatives have already been considered and they would be more blameworthy. In deciding to intervene we are saying that Option A would likely result in more deaths or more harm. Otsuka's PAB thus confirms that we would not be blameworthy if all other alternatives are more blameworthy. Indeed, according to Otsuka there are always least worst options available to us in the dirty hands scenarios for which we cannot be blamed (1998, p. 693). When intervention is deemed just (and thus proportionality and long-term consequences have been deemed acceptable) intervention will be less blameworthy than non-intervention, suggesting that such interventions are permissible.

Accordingly we must accept all of the grim possible realities involved with saving those who can be saved as we are ethically required to do so.[16] "Dirty hands" is a horrible reality we will have to face when deciding whether to intervene post-natural hazard.[17] However, disallowing intervention as a possible response vehicle ensures that people will not be saved by an intervention either and we may be more blameworthy. In sum, the possible killing involved in an intervention, whilst a moral cost, is less blameworthy than not intervening.

7.3.4 Demandingness

The fourth objection to interventions in general is that they are terribly demanding on the intervener. Costs associated with supporting a population's human right to welfare include: (i) the timespan of an intervention; (ii) the economic and human cost; (iii) the political strain put on leaders; (iv) disruption to the lives of the population in the intervening country; (v) animosity of those who received intervention assistance (Walzer, 1995). These are all high costs for supporting a population's human right to welfare.

In addition to the demandingness of the interference, there is also the issue of stabilisation and reconstruction and thus the demandingness of recovery. The "in and quickly out" strategy is not always possible because (a) there may be no institutional or human resources left after the intervention upon which to base a reconstruction, (b) the killing might continue once interveners leave, and (c) the state has disintegrated (Walzer, 2002, p. 7). Disaster relief projects are estimated to have cost the global economy $20 billion per year from 2000 to 2010 (IMF Survey, 2012). In addition, some military operations have maintained a presence in foreign countries for decades thus adding huge financial burdens to the intervening country. This is a huge allocation of resources with little or no direct benefit to the intervening country.

Demandingness is an ethical issue separate to political or economic implications. Most branches of consequentialism subscribe to the rule of utility maximisation. However, it is not clear whose utility matters most or how we go about maximizing utility in dynamic and ever changing scenarios.[18] To illustrate, the provision of tents to those displaced from the L'Aquila earthquake brought about a safe, warm and dry consequence for those whose homes were destroyed. If we look at the same situation and capabilities maximisation, the people affected are anxious about their ability to survive the cold winters. Hence, there seems to be a consistent and never-ending list of requirements necessary to bring about ethical ends for those affected by a natural hazard.[19]

While interventions in many cases may be demanding, I am not arguing that intervention is a tool to be used regularly. Instead, it should be seen as one option for the international community by which it can uphold claims of sovereignty (see Chapter 8) and defend the human right to welfare. Intervening will be demanding and may drain economic and political resources. Understandably, many leaders would be loath to risk economic, political and military stability if previous interventions have turned out poorly. However, developing an intervention policy will ensure that (a) interventions are the exception and not the rule and (b) that any intervention can be done in such a way, and with such international agreement, that no one country's resources will be used disproportionately. Hence, through the establishment of a framework for when natural hazard intervention is morally required we can establish the parameters as to when and how such an intervention will be carried out.[20]

It can also be argued that the moral urgency of providing food to the hungry or shelter to the homeless after a natural hazard is the same as the moral urgency of responding to a massacre. Being virtuous and upholding moral imperatives is difficult. Taking the hard decision to use force and possibly harm people is never an excuse to suspend "the struggle to be virtuous" (Fixdal & Smith, 1998, p. 287). Accordingly, intervention for natural hazards will be demanding but that is not a moral reason not to intervene.

However, the duty to intervene to save those affected by a natural hazard is no more demanding in itself than is the duty to save those affected by conflict. Creating a norm for natural hazard intervention will increase the number of occasions in which an intervention may be carried out. This does not mean that the number of occasions in which an intervention *should* be carried out will increase.

7.3.5 Political will

There are also some who believe that the political will for an intervention is too much to expect from the international community. In fact, high-level debates on the topic of intervention for natural hazard have concluded that non-intervention, and concentration on diplomacy and non-forceful arrangements, is the most appropriate method of response. The original architects of the Responsibility to Protect doctrine assumed natural hazards should be included as triggers for international intervention (Axworthy, 2008). However, when ratified, RtoP did not include natural hazards because there was not enough political will internationally to support their inclusion (see Section 6.2.4). It can thus be argued that no matter what should be done to support those suffering from a natural hazard, we will simply not garner enough support to create, let alone initiate, an intervention.

More recently, in 2006, the United Nation's International Law Commission published the *Draft Articles on Protection of Persons in Event of Disasters* (United Nations, 2016). As discussions progressed, more considerations were added to the draft document. In 2010, one focus was "the primary responsibility of the affected state, due consideration to sovereignty and non-intervention" (Tokunaga, 2014, p. 51). In 2011, drafters focused on including issues associated with "(1) the responsibility of the affected state to seek assistance where its national response capacity is exceeded; (2) the duty of the affected state not to arbitrarily withhold its consent to external assistance; and (3) the right to offer assistance in the international community" (Tokunaga, 2014, p. 53). Eventually these points were incorporated into Articles of the framework – state consent and support of state sovereignty being key (Tokunaga, 2014, p. 55). The parties to the ILC discussion (for the most part) rejected the idea that there was an international duty to assist when a state was not acting on its duties to the affected people (Tokunaga, 2014, p. 54). Political will was once again against the development of natural hazard intervention policy, even when basic human welfare is at stake.

The most expected objection to military intervention is that intervention would cost more to "us" than it would to help "them". Furthermore, we could not guarantee that our interventions to help those affected would actually create long-term stability in the region. There is therefore very little political will to intervene, even if people are suffering. This objection to interventions weighs domestic interests and duties to domestic citizens against those of distant others.

However, we cannot suspend our ethical ideals because garnering support for an intervention would take too much effort. Walzer argues that "supreme emergencies" do not justify abhorrent action, even though he does argue that our ethics may be different in "supreme emergencies" (2004, p. 48). Likewise, ignoring the needs of humans suffering through a "supreme emergency" when we are in a position to help them cannot be ignored. Political will is a difficult thing to rouse. However, we must at least attempt to amend societal norms so that they fit with our ethical ideals. We must work to avoid the death or destruction of innocence (Walzer, 2004). Accordingly, political will must drive both the development and adoption of natural hazard intervention policy.

7.4 Conclusion

In this chapter, I argued that a natural hazard intervention policy is both appropriate and morally required. I set out the parameters of such a policy first by explaining that preparedness is vital to an ethical natural hazard response. When domestic responders are adequately prepared they provide better support. Likewise, if appropriate planning is done in advance of a disaster the international community will be in a position to provide better and timely assistance to those whose governments are unable or unwilling to do so.

Second, I used the Just War Criteria to establish the foundation for a policy for natural hazard intervention. I discussed inability/unwillingness to respond, just cause, proportionality, last resort, right authority, right intention, and long-term consequences of an intervention. I argued that each is a necessary condition for intervention; together the criteria are sufficient to justify an intervention. Using these criteria also helps to establish a practical policy which places the welfare of affected humans at its core.

Finally, in Section 7.3, I discussed the objections to intervention, namely the threat of imperialism, long-term effects of an intervention, dirty hands, demandingness and the lack of political will. Just as there are barriers to the effective provision of assistance in the face of humanitarian emergencies, they will be barriers to intervention for a natural hazard response. (I discuss the strongest objection, sovereignty, in the next chapter.) However, if the objections to intervention in humanitarian emergencies can be disregarded or overcome than they must equally be disregarded or overcome in natural hazard scenarios.

In sum, there is an ethical way forward for the development and implementation of natural hazard intervention policy. Utilising the seven criteria set out in Section 7.2 will help us to determine a just process of intervention commencement. When utilised correctly, systematically and universally the objections to intervention cause less of a concern. Indeed, natural hazard intervention policy is possible and must be created.

Notes

1 In other situations a government may be unwilling to consent to offers of assistance being delivered to their affected country for operational reasons. This denial of assistance may be appropriate if, for example, it is based on the concern that operational and logistical efforts will be overwhelmed by assets superfluous to need.

2 Shue provides an example: "If preventable starvation occurs as an effect of a decision not to prevent it, the starvation is caused by, among other things, the decision not to prevent it. Passive infanticide is still infanticide" (1980, p. 98).

Indeed, if death from lack of basic necessities is preventable, we have a moral obligation to prevent such death.

3 Unable national governments should be understood more along the lines of failed states as discussed in 7.2.1.

4 See discussion in Section 1.1 for the social construction of disasters.

5 This distinction between killing, letting die and preventing people from being saved is also helpful in explaining why my argument is not applicable to intervening in situations of extreme poverty. Hasner explains that intervening to save someone from a *particular* death is a benefit to that person because it is a preventative harm (1999). By contrast, feeding those in extreme poverty will not prevent a person from suffering any harm of that type. Whilst the people suffering both incidents are experiencing harm, these are different harms just as killing and letting die are different (though still harms). So, whilst not supporting those in poverty is unethical, it is a different type of harm than I discuss within this analysis.

6 Beyond this distinction between doing and allowing, a harm occurs where barriers to international assistance are *created* by a national government. In natural hazard scenarios, an agent did not trigger the sequence of events that resulted in people's low welfare. Hence on Foot's analysis preventing aid would be *allowing* harm. Woollard argues, though, that Foot's analysis does not go far enough and must account for situations in which preventing aid *sustains* harm (Woollard, 2012, p. 455).

7 When an intervention is discussed at the international level, acting quickly (and therefore carrying out a coercive intervention) may save more lives (Conces, 2001, p. 142). People need not be on the brink of death for there to be a just cause for intervention. Simply, the expectation that a situation will continue to deteriorate if assistance is not addressed quickly is enough to qualify as a just cause for intervention.

8 According to the Carnegie Commission on Preventing Deadly Conflicts, military interventions themselves may be the most appropriate mechanism for preventing conflict escalation and thus diplomatic discussions should assume the possibility of a military component (Fixdal & Smith, 1998, p. 302). Scholars have found that the use of force may be ethically justified even if illegal under international law (Massingham, 2009, p. 825). Military intervention may prevent the escalation of a disaster and hence the use of force is at least a viable response to the escalation of destruction and disaster post-natural hazard.

9 I argue that the act of intervening will be just if it meets the criteria set out in this chapter, not that the intervention itself, once forces are present in the disaster area, will be just. This is why I refer to my policy as jus ad interventum. Note the distinction between jus ad bello and jus in bellum (Walzer, 2006).

10 Walzer has suggested that unilateral action may be morally acceptable in situations that require quick action, but we know from recent examples (Iraq and Afghanistan) that there may be fallout from unilateral action (1995, 2002, 2006, p. 107).

11 NATO and/or a coalition of the willing as occurred before the invasion of Iraq in 2003 would not have the right authority to intervene in a disaster post-natural hazard as I have described. It would not be backed by the authority of the United Nations and, accordingly would not have the backing of the authoritative body within international relations. NATO and a coalition of the willing are thus not possible legitimate authorities for deciding to intervene as it represents only a specific group of countries.

12 It is worth considering the creation of a separate body to organise and deploy for naturalhazard interventions which has a direct communication and authority line to the authorizing body within the United Nations. However, the ERC may be

an appropriate model upon which a new natural hazard intervention decision-making body should be formed.

13 There are other long-term implications that should also be considered: environmental and non-human animal. These are controversial and unnecessary to discuss as this work concentrates on the *human* right to welfare.

14 Any extra, external assistance without consent can overwhelm responders. In scenarios where a government is unable or unwilling to provide assistance to its people, the decision to intervene must involve coordination with multiple foreign governments and should consider whether the issues faced by an affected population warrant interference. Only then is it that interference without consent can be considered (Holzgrefe, 2003, p. 18; Archibugi, 2004).

15 Refer to Section 7.2.2 for context on the killing versus letting die distinction.

16 Furthermore, there are possible grim realities involved with saving those who can be saved even with the best preparation possible (Zack, 2011).

17 Use of force without due consideration of the individuals likely to be affected is no longer the norm. The interveners first must consider what effect the use of force will have on the local population (Kaldor, 2010, p. 137).

18 See the demandingness of contractualism in emergency situations in Ashford (2003, pp. 280–284).

19 Furthermore, if maximizing utility continues to be the ultimate end of disaster relief, it is very possible that we would be required to devote all energy to relieving the suffering of others. This would be very demanding.

20 Additionally, natural hazards create unstable environments and, when the emergency is bad enough, disrupt a society's ability to respond to follow-on or subsequent events (World Economic Forum, 2008). However, recent research does suggest that disasters may not impact greatly on political stability (Omelicheva, 2011).

8 The sovereignty objection to natural hazard intervention

The strongest objections to interventions of any kind are based on the idea of state sovereignty. Since the Peace of Westphalia in 1648, the concept of sovereignty has been used to order the international system and justify legitimate political authority within specific, territorially bounded areas. Sovereignty is beneficial to all aspects of societal life: it empowers a self-governing people, through a governing body, to secure a territory from external threats while providing an internal governance structure. The establishment of a system of sovereign states was intended to prevent war and allow for international peace. In more recent times, however, sovereignty has become a contentious issue, used as a defence by national governments against foreign policies and practices.

In 8.1, I explain what it means for a state to be sovereign. The classical definition of sovereignty is "to be the ultimate source of political power within a realm" (Morris, 2000). However, this definition highlights the contentious and problematic aspects of sovereignty. I therefore suggest different ways for supremacy and authority to be understood. In 8.2, I outline why sovereignty is considered worth respecting, i.e., the societal benefits gained from state sovereignty (self-determination, international recognition, political rights, security and cooperation). In 8.3, I describe how the notion of sovereignty can be used to ground objections to my central argument. In 8.4, with the better understanding of sovereignty, I respond to this sovereignty-based objection. I argue that in relevant natural hazards sovereignty and intervention are not in conflict in a way that would make interventions impermissible in these cases. Indeed, interventions can be permissible in relevant natural hazard cases even if we recognise the value of state sovereignty.

8.1 What is sovereignty?

At a fundamental level, sovereignty can be understood as "supreme authority within a territory", or in other words, "the ultimate authority" within a geographically bounded community (James, 1986, p. 5; Philpott, 2010). In this section, I explain three key elements of sovereignty – authority, supremacy and territoriality – and how they are traditionally understood. I argue that two of these elements – authority and supremacy – have not been understood correctly and I therefore propose alternative interpretations.

First, with political authority a government can establish and enforce rules, deliver judgements, and implement rules from external sources (such as international bodies) (Pogge, 1992). Experts disagree on what it is for a state to have political authority. With a traditional view, authority consists of two distinct elements (Raz, 1985, pp. 5–6). According to the first, purely descriptive element, an authority must have the ability to coerce the subjects of the authority and those subjects must have a tendency to acquiesce to the commands of the authority. Now, if this descriptive element of sovereign authority were the only way of understanding authority, dictators who coerced us to follow commands would count as authorities.

This authority must also be legitimate. The authority must have the *right* to make demands and coerce people to follow them and the subjects must have a *duty* to obey the commands. In this way authority is only possible when there is a certain kind of a moral relationship between the government and the governed. By combining the descriptive and moral elements of authority, the state can be legitimate in a way that gives leaders the right to command and subjects a duty to obey.

The second element of sovereignty is supremacy. Unlike other local or supranational forms of political authority, a sovereign state (supposedly) must have *ultimate* or *supreme* political authority: no one has higher authority in any aspect of political or economic rule. All laws, rules and security are established, authorised and enforced at the state level. States have the capacity to overrule local courts and judgements and may choose to disregard regulations made at the international level. For example, Scotland does not have "ultimate" political authority as it must govern based on laws passed in the British Parliament. The Scottish Parliament is not sovereign because it does not have ultimate authority in Scotland.

It is traditionally argued that this political authority must exist at the state level so as to avoid the problem of infinite regress (Krehoff, 2008; Morris, 1998). According to the problem of infinite regress, any hierarchical system of authority must have closure. Because such hierarchical systems cannot have an infinite number of levels, some agent must be the "highest" authority so as to solve disputes and make final decisions (Morris, 1998).

Consider Scotland again. Whilst Scotland's First Minister has authority over the social, political and economic activities which take place within the country, Britain's Parliament may overrule laws which contradict those at national levels of governance. Under traditional interpretations of sovereignty, the United Kingdom is the final authority and thus regress is finite at the level of Parliament. Likewise, the European Union and the United Nations exercise authority over the United Kingdom. However, these governmental powers do not have "ultimate" authority; that supreme authority rests with the national, sovereign government. Hence, the regression of authority upward closes at the state level and sovereignty solves the problem of infinite regress.

Finally, the concept of "bounded" or "territorially-based" sovereignty gives structure to the international state system. Each sovereign controls and works on behalf of a specific piece of land and the peoples who live within it. The international community upholds norms of entrance into the state system. A government's authority within a territory, and therefore its authority to exercise sovereignty, is acknowledged by the international community in most situations. Whilst borders are morally arbitrary they serve a practical function in organizing the international system of states. Accordingly, I will continue to include this aspect of sovereignty in my definition.

I have thus far explained that sovereignty has traditionally been understood to consist of the supreme authority within a given territory. This authority will not only be able to coerce, but will have the moral right to coerce and thus will be legitimate. In what follows, I first critique the current view of legitimacy within the context of state sovereignty and then explain why traditional understandings of supremacy and authority are outdated.

I begin with the practical foundations of traditional, legitimate sovereign authority. Originally, and until quite recently, the priority of the sovereign state system has been peace and security within a territory and peaceful relations with other states, with each state dominating within its own territorial boundaries (Morris, 1998).[1] An international order which sees to it that ultimate authority remains at the state level provides states with a monopoly on the use of force in order to ensure domestic and international peace (Fund for Peace, 2015; Giddens, 2002, pp. 10–18). To that end, it was assumed that sovereign authority only needed to include the descriptive element of legitimacy, namely that of dominance within a territory and a norm of non-intervention into the affairs of other states.

In the post-World War II era, however, human rights became a more important goal (or at least equal) of the sovereign state system than international peace and security. With this normative shift the moral element of legitimacy, namely that the state has a *right* to coerce, became a requirement of sovereign states. (This does not mean that the state is necessarily *just* even if it is legitimate (Peter, 2010).) So, instead of simply perpetuating domestic security, sovereign authority required that states act on their political obligations. Non-interference in the affairs of other states would not be observed if a state did not uphold its moral obligations to citizens. In this way, in exercising authority a sovereign government was acting on its moral authority as well the purely practical (descriptive) terms of authority. The goal around which the sovereign state system is structured has thus transitioned from peace and security within a territory and peaceful relations with other states to an obligation to uphold human rights (Donnelly, 2014).[2]

As an example of this shift towards a moral authority, based on human rights, consider the following. Citizens accept bad treatment where discrimination normally occurs. However, because a morally legitimate government does not have the right to discriminate, people within a discriminating country do not have a duty to adhere. A "sovereign" government whose citizens do not have a responsibility to follow does not have legitimate authority. Therefore, a legitimate government must meet some minimum moral standard.[3] Mere acceptance of the commands of one's government is not enough to make a government legitimate.

I now move to supremacy: traditional understanding and the value and necessity of *limited* authority. Remember, under traditional interpretations of sovereignty, states impose rules and order in their own territories by way of the political authority that is somehow unique to states. As explained earlier, state political authority is said to be unique because it is the *supreme* authority within a given territory. This gives states the authority to make decisions about all political, economic and social matters free from any external interference. Pure domestic coercion would provide the mechanism through which political authority could be exercised.

Now, political authority does indeed require the ability to coerce; however, that ability to coerce is not specific to states. The international community can also be said to have political authority and this is without undermining or contradicting political authority at the state level. The state must yield to global decisions around, say, environmental protection, for reasons of practical enforcement and improvement of global systems (or risk political fallout, a kind of coercion). Likewise, engagement with international trade comes with methods of enforcement including fines and exclusions from discussion-making. Hence the international community has the ability to coerce and can be a legitimate authority.

States are not hindered from exercising their sovereignty by adhering to such global regulations or enforcements. Indeed, there is no problem of infinite regress hindering state sovereignty or a government's ability to govern – there need not be an ultimate authority on all matters for authority to be meaningful. Political authority need only be sufficiently authoritative. Furthermore, an authority that is superior on all matters is simply unrealistic (Morris, 2000). One domestic institution might have more expertise in one area than another domestic institution. Here, the institution with more expertise will also have more authority in that specific area – whether that authority flows from the local or supranational level (Pogge, 1992). Just as you would not want the fire service to make decisions on education, a state cannot possibly be expected to moderate on all aspects of society. Hence authority should and does flow from the institutions with the expertise to carry out the relevant tasks.

So if we accept the idea that there should be a distribution of authority amongst those with the expertise and positioning to make certain decisions, states may not exercise "ultimate" authority. If states did act as "ultimate" authorities, it would likely hinder the development of global policies. State-based authority (solely) thus limits the possibility of engagement necessary for global policy reform. Instead, limited authority at the state level may be a more appropriate way of understanding sovereign authority. With limited authority, states can make all required decisions on issues that affect them and to which they have sufficient expertise. Other decisions will be made by those with a global view and specific expertise. It will also ensure that those making policy do not have the ability to contradict the needs of those in other countries.

I therefore argue for *limited* as opposed to *ultimate* authority as an integral component of sovereignty (Krehoff, 2008). The international community has legitimate authority, for example, over the monetary system; the international system of stock exchanges and currency calculators is not illegitimate because it emanates from bodies across (instead of at the level of) states. Instead, legitimate authority should be wielded by that organisation in a position to deliver desirable outcomes. Sovereign authority may therefore be limited without undermining its legitimacy and/or the benefits gained from sovereignty.

The relationship between the state government and the governed (and the corresponding rights and duties enshrined in that relationship) is not undermined by the fact that the government is not the final authority on certain aspects of political life. A parent's relationship with her child is not diminished by the fact that she does not have final authority over that child's education. Furthermore, the international community may exercise legitimate authority when it is the most appropriate body to deliberate on specific matters.

So, sovereignty may be understood as a territorially bounded political community in line with traditional definitions of sovereignty. However, it only requires limited moral authority within a territory. By understanding sovereignty in this way, infinite regress ceases to be a problem. Also, authority can be exercised by those best placed to provide certain goods or services.

8.2 Benefits of sovereignty

With a more appropriate interpretation of sovereignty, I turn now to why sovereignty is valuable internally and externally to the state (and hence why objections to interventions are based on the primacy of sovereignty). Even sovereignty with limited authority, as I have argued for in this chapter, has several benefits, including self-determination of peoples and international recognition. Additionally, because the state has the power to coerce, sovereignty also accounts for political rights, security and international peace.

8.2.1 Self-determination

First, collective self-determination is the ability of a people to establish a state within which it can govern according to its own political and cultural requirements. In essence, the establishment of a sovereign state empowers a people to be in charge of their own destiny and demonstrates the group's desire for a territorially bounded state. For example, in the aftermath of World War I, many groups of peoples (the Poles, Italians, Romanians and others) sought recognition of their existence as a people and the establishment of states separate from the Hapsburg empire. Ethnic and nationalist groups appealed for national self-determination and campaigned for territorial rights which would allow them to realise their economic and political potential as a self-governing people (Stevenson, 2001; Keylor, 2001, p. 60).

Sovereignty makes self-determination possible. In a post-World War I era, the Poles, Italians and other self-determining people were able to rule over a territory. When nations of people do not have the ability to make decisions on their collective lives, they are constricted by the will of others without the understanding or expertise necessary to legitimately govern with authority. Hence, if nations are not sovereign, they cannot be self-determining. Self-determination is thereby an important benefit of sovereignty as it empowers people to live under a government that recognises its cultural and political needs.

8.2.2 International recognition and resulting non-domination

Another benefit of sovereignty is international recognition: the acceptance by other sovereign states of a government's right to rule over a territorially bounded community and the agreement of those same states to interact with the state as an equal (United Nations, 2015, Article 2). As equal participants in the international state system, states are assured that they will not be dominated by another state without (at least) first obtaining authority from the international community. Furthermore, when a state is internationally recognised, self-determining people have an outlet for their collective will. Recognition matters because it empowers a sovereign state to realise its future (Iser, 2013). Accordingly, national governments act on the authority of those self-determining people on external and internal matters of state. States are therefore able to govern within their territories on the will of their own people, free from external domination.

8.2.3 Coercion: Political rights, security and cooperation

Coercion is a means by which one's intentions are forced onto another's actions. At the state level, coercion may involve the use of physical force via the police or military. It can also include things like tax collection through which funds and services are distributed back to the population and through which society is able to flourish (Fabre, 2012, p. 27). State coercion is also one important means through which a government imposes societal norms on a population. Individuals within a state willingly give up certain freedoms and responsibility in deference to that state. Through coercion, laws can be enforced and thus, it is argued, order is possible.

Order, of course, is valuable to those who live within a state. In exchange for an individual's freedom, the state agrees to provide political rights, security and cooperation. This agreement ensures a society's civility and the people's continued cooperation with the state and other co-citizens (Lloyd & Sreedhar, 2014).

One benefit of coercion is political rights: entitlements which enable human persons to live freely within the legal apparatus of the state and include such things as free speech, the right to vote, freedom of assembly and so forth (United Nations Enable, 2004; United Nations, 1976). Political rights are not possible without the state's ability to arrest or detain those who would stop others from exercising their freedoms. Indeed, states enforce rights through the use of force where necessary.

A second benefit of coercion is security. In exchange for following the rules set out by a sovereign government, individuals should expect a certain level of security. The state's ability to coerce is linked to its legitimate control of violence within the state and, if necessary, toward foreign enemies.[4] Because the state maintains the legitimate control of violence, it can use force to coerce and punish those who threaten state security.

In accordance with international law, a state has the authority to use force and this is commonly accepted (United Nations, 2015). Accordingly, people are unwilling to threaten state security in general and they will accept the state's claim on the control of violence. So, with the ability to coerce a sovereign state is able to provide security to its people in the form of local and national law enforcement or reinforcing flood barriers ahead of hurricane season.

The state is also the primary provider of defence against foreign domination. The state maintains a military for warfighting and protective response against external enemies. In a non-military capacity, the state maintains an official diplomatic presence to defend the interests of the domestic population. Through the legitimate use of violence and ability to coerce, sovereign states provide individuals with expected levels of security.

A final benefit of coercion discussed in this chapter is cooperation. State sovereignty creates an environment in which citizens can cooperate towards a mutually desired society. Cooperation occurs because we trust that the state will act on our behalf if someone does not follow the rules. Those who do not cooperate with the mutually agreed-upon rules, for example, those who commit a burglary or fraud, will be punished. Likewise, each person cooperates with the rules of the society because each person wants to reap the rewards of a mutually supportive society – public goods such as education or roads. Thus, sovereignty is valuable because of the public goods that result from the establishment and enforcement of these rules.

And so, the benefits of a sovereign state's use of coercion are political rights, security and public goods. Cooperation and adherence to shared norms of practice lead to stable and productive states and allow for satisfactory individual lives. Sovereignty, through its ability to coerce, therefore offers a means of achieving mutually beneficial cooperative goals.

8.3 Sovereignty-based objections to interventions post-natural hazard

Sovereignty can therefore be beneficial and worth maintaining. The over-riding theme of any sovereignty-based objection to natural hazard intervention would be that external interventions undermine state sovereignty and thereby threaten the benefits gained from it. When a foreign government interferes in the affairs of a national government, it is interfering with the desires of a self-determining people. By extension, the foreign interveners are not respecting the state's right of non-interference and thus not recognising its equal status in the international community of states. Most importantly, if a state's authority is undermined it loses its ability to effectively coerce its people and therefore to provide political rights, security and cooperation.

Using the Cyclone Nargis (2008) case study, there are clear sovereignty-based reasons as to why the international community objected to intervention. Diplomacy is and should continue to be the central mechanism for the international community to provide assistance when a national government is unable or unwilling to provide assistance to its people as it maintains balance within the international system of sovereign states. Also, any intervention for the purpose of natural hazard response can be seen as aggression against a sovereign country and hence an act of war.

In general, some argue that international peace and security – a good made possible by sovereign state coercion – is best served by *not* using force and creating more conflict in the world. Hence, any intervention would damage the peace and stability of the country receiving the "aid" as well as those countries which would be drawn into the "fight" to deliver assistance in the aftermath of a natural hazard against the wishes of the affected state (Asia-Pacific Centre for the Responsibility to Protect, 2008). Accordingly, any intervention into a sovereign state could lead to a destabilisation of the international state system made possible by sovereignty.

Instead, the most appropriate mechanism for addressing response needs after a natural hazard is to adhere to sovereign norms of non-intervention and rely on diplomacy. If all states are equal in the international system of states, then states should be able to negotiate with each other in order to provide for the needs of those affected by a natural hazard and those who would suffer from the knock-on effects of the emergency. Proponents of diplomacy further suggest that bringing an end to human suffering through peaceful means would lead to assistance being delivered to those affected faster and more effectively (Thakur, 2008). Hence diplomacy, and not intervention, is the most appropriate mechanism by which to get assistance to natural-hazard-affected humans.

The most extreme argument against intervention post-natural hazard is that intervention can be seen as an act of war the goal of which is to conquer, destroy or at least drastically change the political and social environment. An intervention in certain scenarios, it is argued, would have established the intervening power as the highest authority. If we had intervened in Myanmar after Cyclone Nargis, we would have bypassed a sovereign government and undermined the generals' ability to respond to the disaster effectively. After foreign aid was allowed into Myanmar, some humanitarian workers claimed that mass starvation was not the problem it was thought to be (Cohen, 2008). The national government may therefore have been correct that external assistance was unnecessary. Hence, an intervention would have been a violation of Myanmar's sovereign right to administer internal matters and would have ignored the political decisions made by self-determining people as to the structure and political norms of their government.

Furthermore, a natural hazard intervention could result in a new kind of colonialism (Axworthy, 2008). Even when sovereignty involves only limited authority, a forced domination of a people within a geographically bounded space will undermine the legitimate authority of the state government. This will have cascading effects on the international system of states and their ability to rule within their own territories. Hence, the security that sovereignty allows for would be jeopardised.

The potential loss of international peace and security, political rights, and security should cause us hesitation when deciding whether or not to intervene. However, there are counter-arguments to these objections critics of intervention have often ignored. In the next section, I explain why an intervention for natural hazard response is still permissible in relevant cases despite claims of the sanctity of sovereignty (Chopra & Weiss, 1992).

8.4 Responding to the objections

In this section, I first argue that reasons against interventions cannot be based on the sanctity of sovereignty. In particular, in situations where there is a failed state or where a state is unresponsive, sovereignty is already diminished and thus cannot be the reason for not intervening. In Section 8.4.2, I argue that the international community can provide the same goods as sovereign states and hence the international community has the obligation to do so when a state is not acting on its sovereign duties. Finally, in Section 8.4.3, I argue that, in defending sovereignty, critics of my argument have ignored the fact that the human right to a minimal level of welfare is more important than sovereign authority.

8.4.1 Unable or unwilling to assist own people

In Section 8.1, I explained that two essential elements of legitimate political authority are the ability to coerce and the right to be obeyed which must be based on the legitimacy of the sovereign state. This means that if a state lacks either the ability to coerce or legitimate authority to make demands on the people, then the state cannot be sovereign. If this is right, then there can be no objection to intervention in cases in which a state either has no power to coerce or it lacks moral legitimacy to govern insofar as sovereignty is concerned.

With that in mind, I begin by arguing that interventions into failed states in the aftermath of a natural hazard do not conflict with norms of sovereignty. Failed states do not have the ability to coerce and thus they fail to have political authority. Second, I argue that states unresponsive to offers of assistance are not carrying out their sovereign duties to provide for the security of their people; they are therefore not legitimate and thus have no right to be obeyed.[5] As a consequence, sovereignty cannot be used as an objection for natural hazard interventions in these types of scenarios.

Consider first a situation in which the government (and possibly the economic and social structures) of a sovereign state have collapsed leaving a political vacuum. The people, while still at least in principle self-determining, no longer have a mechanism through which to carry out their will as there is no state acting on their behalf. A collapse of a government would qualify a country as either a fragile or, more likely, a "failed state" (Fund for Peace, 2015). According to the *Failed State Index,* those acting to promote national recovery will need to revive the "'core five' institutions: military, police, civil service, the system of justice and leadership" (The Fund for Peace, 2015). A total state collapse means that a government is no longer self-determining and there is therefore no sovereignty to be respected.

In 2010, Haiti ranked 11th in the world on the Failed State Index (The Fund for Peace, 2010). State legitimacy and human rights are two indicators used to establish a state's ranking. Haiti's high rank on this scale can be put down to its high crime rate and endemic corruption. It also has low citizen confidence which often means that the state is unable to exercise its coercive powers including its authority to collect taxes (The Fund for Peace, 2014, p. 11). As for human rights, failed states are characterised as having widespread state-administered political oppression (The Fund for Peace, 2014, p. 13).

When the earthquake hit Haiti in 2010, it was already in political and economic upheaval. With this chaos, it lacks legitimate political authority because it does not have the ability to coerce and thus there is no (or at least diminished) sovereignty to be respected. Those providing assistance in Haiti did bypass the government in some ways but the international community did not undermine the sovereignty of the country, as the country was not sovereign in the first place.

The second type of situation in which intervention may be permissible insofar as sovereignty is concerned are those cases where a government is unwilling to provide for the needs of its people.[6] Assistance may be refused because of inflated egos or an inability to see the true status of the situation due to a "fog of war" (Kiesling, 2001). According to Robert McNamara, the "fog of war" is when conflicting messages, fear, time delays, egos and lack of knowledge cloud the judgement of policy makers (The Fog of War, 2003). It can also refer to a disregard for the suffering of the affected people or to resistance to outside influences in order to maintain tighter control over the government.

As I argued in Section 8.1, a state must have moral legitimacy in order to be sovereign. If a state is unwilling to meet a minimal moral threshold to its people, it can be said to lack legitimacy. It follows that if a state lacks legitimacy it does not have political authority and hence the state is not sovereign. In effect, it has voided the terms of the agreement under which citizens accept state coercion.

We can take an unwillingness to respond to offers of assistance or declining offers of necessary assistance as non-adherence to the norms and obligations of sovereign statehood. According to Article 40 of the Draft Articles on Responsibility of States for Internationally Wrongful Acts, states have a responsibility to maintain the "peremptory norm of general international law" (International Law Commission, 2001/2008). Prohibitions of genocide, slavery, torture are such norms of international law and thus adherence to basic human rights can be reasonably grouped here under the heading of "Aggravated State Responsibility" (Breau, 2016; International Law Commission, 2001/2008). In an emergency, an affected population will have certain claims – or rather, have certain human rights – which the government has a duty to fulfil. A state which does not request necessary aid is not providing for the needs or security of its people which are central to its claim of sovereign authority.

A "serious breach" of human rights, as would be necessary to invoke Article 40, would involve systemic or significant violations of human rights (and thus is in line with my argument that intervention for violations of the human right to welfare in the aftermath of a natural hazard will likely be a rare occurrence) (International Law Commission, 2001/2008). Unwillingness to provide for the needs of its people is a violation of a state's sovereign duty to provide for the security and rights of its people. Breau argues that even preventing aid, as discussed in Section 7.2.2, could constitute a "violation of a peremptory norm of international law" (Breau, 2016, p. 88). With this, I argue that a state is not legitimate when it does not fulfil its sovereign duties to maintain the norm of human rights and therefore sovereignty is not present in a way that it can be violated.[7]

In this section, I have argued that there are two domestically focused reasons why the sovereignty-based objection to intervention fails. I first explained that failed states are not exercising sovereignty in the usual way and hence an intervention is not a violation of sovereignty. I next discussed how countries which reject assistance are not upholding the norms of the sovereign state system and hence cannot be said to be acting on legitimate political authority. Accordingly, the international community may act with authority in these types of scenarios.

8.4.2 International community can provide public goods

A further reason to reject the sovereignty-based objection to intervention is that the intervening global community can provide the public goods usually provided by sovereign states when a state is unable or unwilling to do so themselves. Actually, the international community has the ability to (and already does) coerce and provide security and public goods.

First, the international community coerces states to adhere to international norms and uphold human rights. For example, states adhere to international regulations regarding war crimes and conflict. States use of the Oslo guidelines, even if it is only limited use, demonstrates a tacit acceptance of international coercion in the realm of natural hazard relief (Multinational, 2007). This acceptance of international guidelines by states means that the international community can assist those individual states which are unable to assist themselves.

Second, the international community is capable of providing social and physical security to states which would be necessary in the aftermath of a natural hazard. In Haiti during the 2010 earthquake, peacekeeping forces were trying to restore political stability by setting a policing agenda and suppressing violence where possible (United Nations, 2013, p. 7). The international community continues to provide for the political stability and physical security of average Haitians, despite perceptions that it is acting as an occupying or at least interfering force (United Nations, 2013, p. 7). Here the international community has a legitimate authority to support the needs of those affected and restore state authority to rule.

While it is the public goods made possible by sovereignty that are valuable, the international community can (and will) provide these goods when a state is unable to do so. Most often the delivery of such public goods happens in times of conflict or war. Despite the difference in circumstances surrounding conflicts and natural hazards, in both emergencies humans require security as well as basic goods such as food, water and shelter. The international community can and does provide public goods in emergency situations without calling into question the sovereignty of the state affected. The international community does have the authority to coerce in specific emergency situations when mandated by the international system of states. Equally, then, the benefits gained from state sovereignty cannot be used as an objection to intervention when the emergency is triggered by a natural hazard.

8.4.3 Human right to (minimum) welfare is important

Thus far, I have explained why we can reject the sovereignty-based objection to intervention. As a further response to criticisms of intervention, consider that interventions for natural hazard response may be permissible because the human right to basic welfare is more important than claims of sovereignty. Indeed, at a certain point in a disaster, discussions regarding whether sovereignty will be breached by an intervention should become secondary to concerns over the loss of life and the amount of suffering resulting from the disaster. It is indeed reasonable to suggest that sovereignty may be infringed if there are more important human rights at stake (Dobos, 2012, pp. 35–36). In this section, I argue that the sovereignty-based objection to intervention in relevant scenarios can be rejected because the human right to a minimal level of welfare is more important than the political rights made possible by sovereignty. Indeed, without the basic minimum goods associated with the human right to welfare political rights will be unachievable.

Once again, I am particularly interested in the human right to minimum welfare – which includes access to food, water, basic shelter and basic medical care – as being fundamental to the enjoyment of all other human rights. The right to these goods has the highest priority because without minimum welfare, political and economic rights are impossible (Nickel, 2013, p. 24; Shue, 1980). Take for example the right to education. If a group of people is being deprived of an education for any number of reasons, this violates their human rights. However, if this group is also being deprived of food and shelter, the food and shelter must "trump" or, rather, be addressed first, before the right to education (Nickel, 1987). People need to eat before they are physically able to learn. Hence the human right to basic levels of welfare – making sure that people have food – is more important than getting an education and exercising certain political rights.

Arguably then, human rights are the central guide for fair and peaceful coexistence in the global society; sovereignty is secondary. The peace supposedly made possible by sovereignty requires that people's basic needs are being met. Hence basic welfare must be prioritised over sovereignty in order for any of the goods of sovereignty to be realised. If humans are hungry, for example, they will defy curfews and risk imprisonment for stealing in order to obtain food. If people are not able to participate in society (because of hunger, disease or homelessness), than the political right to do so is irrelevant.

Hence sovereignty is less important than the human right to basic welfare because the benefits gained from sovereignty are not as important as food, water, shelter and basic security. As explained in Chapter 4, an intervention is required when people are denied the goods associated with basic welfare in the aftermath of a natural hazard. Hence, any objection to intervention based on sovereignty must consider the impact non-intervention will have on the human rights of those affected. Indeed, human rights are of a higher priority than all other political considerations including sovereignty.

8.5 Intervention can bolster sovereignty

In Section 8.2, I discussed an intervention's capacity to restore domestic security and political rights. Taking this point further, an intervention can be said to help restore sovereignty in the aftermath of a natural hazard. I argue that intervention can be justified on the grounds that it would restore international stability within the sovereign state system.

Chapter VII, Article 42 of the UN Charter authorises the use of force to "maintain or restore international peace and security" (United Nations, 2013). Allowing the systemic abuse of human rights undermines the system upon which human rights are established. When crimes that "shock the conscience" of humankind (genocide, human rights abuses and other crimes against humanity) occur, they threaten the balance of international peace and security. Likewise, the justification used for breaching sovereignty via the Responsibility to Protect is that we have a duty to those affected over and above those duties to maintain state sovereignty (Haider, 2013).

To illustrate, imagine a scenario in which the international community disregards its responsibilities under the UN Charter and the Responsibility to Protect. Failure to intervene to stop various crimes against humanity would suggest that the laws of the international community do not need to be followed. This would undermine current systems of global governance.

Equally, failure to intervene to alleviate human suffering would suggest that sovereignty is more important than the welfare of individual humans. Non-intervention would undermine the reasoning used to justify the implementation of the Responsibility to Protect and therefore call into question the application of RtoP principles in future situations of genocide, human rights abuse and humanitarian emergencies. International peace and security are only possible when global norms and laws are followed. Non-intervention would thereby threaten the balance of international peace and security.

My point in this section is not to argue for intervention on the grounds of human rights abuses as I have done elsewhere. Rather, if we do not intervene in situations where individuals are at risk of death at the hands of their government then we are saying that sovereignty is more important than the peace and security it was intended to create. Evans has argued that overuse of RtoP would bring about an "evaporation" of the new norm for intervention which supersedes the norm of sovereignty (2008). Equally, however, I argue that non-intervention on behalf of those affected by a natural hazard reinforces the norm of non-intervention because of sovereignty. If we want to continue to move forward from arguments in favour of the primacy of sovereignty then we must take a stand on the rights of humans in all types of emergency situations – not just those dictated by RtoP. It follows, then, that deaths caused by natural hazard when a national government is unable or unwilling to provide certain goods undermines international peace and security and thus requires intervention from the international community in the same way as crimes against humanity require intervention.

In sum, non-intervention for disasters post-natural hazard undermines the justification used for intervention in those situations for which RtoP is invoked. Non-intervention in these scenarios for reasons of sovereignty equally throws into question the broader norms established by the UN Charter which were developed to maintain international stability. Hence, in order to maintain international peace and security, natural hazard intervention is required.[8]

8.6 Conclusion

In this chapter, I first explained what sovereignty is: political authority within a geographically bounded area. I then outlined the benefits of sovereignty. These include such things as self-determination, international recognition and, through a sovereign state's ability to coerce, political rights, security and public goods. Indeed, sovereignty provides valuable goods to individuals and offers a mechanism for the maintenance of international order and security.

Because of the benefits gained from sovereignty, it can be argued that intervention is impermissible in certain natural hazard scenarios. Interventions can undermine the wishes of a self-determining people and lead to increased violence and threats to international peace and security. An intervention for natural hazard response could also undermine a state's authority to coerce its people and hence disempower the state's ability to provide public goods such as security and political rights.

In Section 8.4, I responded to these important objections by arguing that in some failed state scenarios and when governments are unwilling to provide for the needs of their people, sovereignty is not the objection to intervention it is sometimes said to be. Sovereignty-based objections to natural hazard intervention misinterpret sovereign authority and its subservience to the goods associated with the human right to minimum welfare. Indeed, sovereignty is not the barrier to intervention it is often argued to be. Those affected by a natural hazard require assistance when their government is unable or unwilling to provide for their needs. It is thereby impractical to disallow an intervention on the grounds of sovereignty, traditionally understood.

Notes

1 International peace and security are only possible when society accepts and adheres to rules set out to order the system of sovereign states. When a state refuses to provide for the needs of its people, it is not adhering to the norms of international sovereign statehood. An intervention can then be said to restore order to and thereby reinforce the organisation of the sovereign state system. Refusing assistance may thereby necessitate intervention for reasons of international stability.

2 For discussion on a state governing without the consent of the governed, see (Luban, 1980, p. 169). For more on the legitimacy of states fighting foreign oppression when it is oppressing its own citizens, see discussion within Doppelt (1978).

3 Nickel has argued that human rights are guarantees of human freedom which must be secured in order for any state to be considered legitimate (2013).

4 See also Giddens (2002, pp. 10–18).

5 See also Breau (2016) who cites Jarrod Wong's article – "Reconstructing the Responsibility to Protect in the wake of Cyclones and Separatism".

6 It is of course possible that assistance is turned down because it will overwhelm the local responders or is simply not needed. A state does not, therefore, automatically qualify for intervention based on a lack of sovereignty because it declines aid.

7 Article 40 of the Draft Articles on Responsibility of States for Internationally Wrongful Acts does not explain how to address such breaches of international norms. Instead, Article 41 of the doctrine states that "States shall cooperate to bring to an end through lawful means any serious breach with the meaning of Article 40" (International Law Commission, 2001/2008). Cooperation is appropriate and may come in the form of diplomacy or organised sanctions. However, I contend that this may provide the legal and normative justification to do what is necessary to provide goods associated with the human right to welfare to those affected by a natural hazard when their national government is unable or unwilling to do so. However, intervention for the purpose of natural hazard response is not necessarily "lawful means" and so the central issue of this book remains open. A policy or legal decision which particularly focuses on post-natural hazard intervention is still required.

8 Dobos defends paternalistic intervention (2012, pp. 44–45).

9 Conclusion

Herein, I have argued that there are cases in which we are morally required to intervene in the aftermath of a natural hazard when a government is unable or unwilling to provide necessary support to its people. I argued that the human right to welfare is just as important in the aftermath of a natural hazard as it is under normal circumstances and thus the international community has a duty to respond. At a minimum, we are morally required to develop a policy that guides intervention which accounts for the duties associated with the right to welfare in post-natural hazard circumstances.

To that end, I have argued for the creation of a natural hazard military intervention policy. We already have military intervention policy for genocide and large-scale human rights abuses. There is no fundamental moral reason why we are not prepared to intervene for those affected by a natural hazard as well, when the incident is such that the human right to welfare is not being supported.

Indeed, the international community must prepare for a situation in which it is necessary to protect the human right to welfare of those affected. I thus explained that the creation of a policy which ensures that humans have a basic level of welfare in the aftermath of a natural hazard is ethically required and appropriate. The human right to welfare creates a duty for the international community to act on behalf of the affected. I argued in Chapter 4 that grounding the human right to welfare in our humanity is necessary so as to account for the universality, high-priority nature of rights. Creating a universal policy based on the human right to welfare grounded in our humanity gives us an opportunity to provide assistance to all those in need of post-natural hazard assistance.

This is not to say that the international community should intervene in the aftermath of every natural hazard. Each disaster must be weighed on its own merit, considering if and how basic provisions are being distributed, and in its own time against a set of criteria. Political will, capacity to respond (say if there are many emergencies at the same time), and the ability of a national government to support its own people with only non-force assistance from the international community, must all be weighed. However, this does not imply or justify the delivery of assistance to some but not others. Instead, we must understand when the international community is morally required to intervene militarily and make every effort to adhere to the responsibilities stemming from the human right to welfare.

Of course, there are many concerns about an intervention policy as I suggest. As explained in Chapter 7, the possibility of imperialism, long-term effects of an intervention, dirty hands, the demandingness of an intervention and the lack of political will are all possible objections to my central argument. However, as argued throughout, intervention is appropriate and required in some cases. The Just War Criteria outlined in 7.2 offer a morally sound way of approaching natural hazard response.

The reader will note that I accept that my suggestions will be politically difficult and may cause a loss of innocent lives. These are hurdles to a military intervention policy for post-natural hazard. These hurdles are not, however, moral justification for not developing an international policy for intervention. Likewise, sovereignty is not a moral barrier to a post-natural hazard intervention.

The moral justification I have provided depends on the human right to welfare and the fact that there are associated duties regardless of an affected person's geographical location. Accordingly, the international community has a duty to (at least prepare to) supply the goods associated with this right to welfare in the aftermath of a natural hazard. The implications of following and integrating my argument into global disaster policy will be strenuous and cumbersome. However, intervention is a morally sound and thus required mechanism for supporting those affected by a natural hazard in some situations.

So as to prepare the international community to act on its second-order responsibilities to protect the human right to welfare in the aftermath of a natural hazard, I recommend the development of an international natural hazard intervention policy and response plan. First, though, I do not suggest the inclusion of natural hazards into the Responsibility to Protect (RtoP). As others have argued, such an inclusion would possibly undermine the political will to use RtoP in cases of genocide, human rights abuse and humanitarian emergencies (Thakur, 2008; Evans, 2008). Whilst I do not think there is a finite amount of political will in the world, I would not want to take that chance. Likewise, I do not here propose the development of specific international law. Very recent attempts at creating laws which account for the international community's second-order responsibilities have failed (Tokunaga, 2014). Another attempt, so soon after the failed attempt, would be unproductive; a policy for natural hazard intervention would be sufficient. Instead, I suggest the creation and implementation of a separate natural hazard intervention norm and associated policy which can be debated on its own merits without calling into question the continuing validity of RtoP.

Considering the international community's adamant position that disaster assistance should be the primary responsibility of the national government affected, I do not believe it wise to try to develop an intervention policy as argued for herein at an international forum or through international legal structures.[1] Instead, one country will have to initiate such a norm development and petition for it at the international level. Indeed, such a policy as I suggest will only be possible if there is a continued normative shift away from the primacy of sovereignty and toward the primacy of human rights in international politics. The norm that would develop should recognise the international community's responsibility to respond to violations of the human right to welfare in the aftermath of a natural hazard where a national government is unable or unwilling to support its people. This method was successful for Canada's International Commission on Intervention and State Sovereignty when they developed the RtoP doctrine as it was then adopted by the United Nations (ICISS, 2001). Furthermore, to be consistent with cosmopolitan justice, an ethical policy for natural hazard intervention must be established with broad buy-in from national governments. Only then will any policy as I argue for be built on the right authority (Section 7.2.5). The coordinator of such a project will need to bring about consensus from a majority of the international community on two distinct issues: (1) that it is the international community's obligation to protect the human right to welfare and ensure that humans have access to basic goods of food, water, shelter and basic medical care; (2) that when a national government is unable or unwilling to ensure such access in the aftermath of a natural hazard, an intervention is morally required.[2]

Once a consensus has established that the associated policy is necessary it should be brought to the international community as a finished product in the form of a policy document, again, similar to the process by which Canada submitted the work of the ICISS. At this stage, with a policy decided, the international community will be prepared to act on their duties in the midst of any future related incidents. What is left is to decide what will trigger the use of such a plan and how it will be operationalised.

There will likely be a large number of people suffering which will represent a large-scale human rights violation and thus a just cause for intervention may be determined (Section 7.2.2). A respected, well-networked international disaster organisation should be given the authority to decide when an intervention is required. OCHA responds to humanitarian emergencies and thus has the practical experience to determine on-the-ground priorities, coordinate and address concerns/objections to an intervention raised by those in the international community contributing to the response and develop the appropriate response. Hence, I argue that a sub-office of OCHA should be developed for the coordination of multilateral agreement that an intervention is necessary in line with the Just War Criteria set out in Section 7.2 and to be included in the actual policy. That office can then pull from its own resources and expertise to carry out the intervention.

Once it has been decided that an intervention is necessary, the right authority must do the intervening. An intervention would need to be carried out under the control of the Office for the Coordination of Humanitarian Affairs (OCHA) together with the Emergency Response Coordinator (ERC) (see Section 7.2.5). As OCHA and the ERC already have the authority to manage international disaster relief, they are the obvious choice to manage or at least liaise with the militaries that will deploy in response to a natural hazard. Such a military force should be similar in scope and mission to that of the "white helmets" suggested by cosmopolitans as an international military force whose mission is to respond to international peacekeeping missions (Archibugi, 2004).

In sum, the crux of my argument and the driving force behind this research is the idea that all humans, no matter where they live or disaster they face, have a human right to welfare. We are therefore duty-bound to make sure that, when preventable events (meaning the resultant disaster from a natural hazard) threaten this basic human right, we are at least prepared to respond. A natural hazard intervention policy will offer us a jus ad interventum – a pre-established structure and criteria for engaging in a just military intervention.

Notes

1 In 2007, the International Federation of the Red Cross established the *International Disaster Response Laws* and received unanimous support from the parties to the Geneva Convention (IFRC, 2007). These laws firmly established the role of "domestic" responders and the associated national government. Likewise, from 2007 to 2014, participants of various panels of the UN's International Law Commission decided that disaster relief should remain solely the responsibility of states (see also Section 7.3.5) (Tokunaga, 2014). This decision was made after several attempts to bring international disaster relief legislation together at the global level.

2 Broad consensus-building will thus ensure that the policy resulted from a right intention (Section 7.2.6) and a right authority (Section 7.2.5) in the development stages.

Bibliography

Aisch, G. & Lai, K.K.R., 2017. The Conflicts Along 1,172 Miles of the Dakota Access Pipeline. *The New York Times*, 20 March. https://www.nytimes.com/interactive/2016/11/23/us/dakota-access-pipeline-protest-map.html

Alexander, A., 2003. Bentham, Rights and Humanity: A Fight in Three Rounds. *Journal of Bentham Studies*, 6, pp. 1-18. DOI:10.14324/111.2045-757X.019.

Alexander, D., 2015. Disaster and Emergency Planning for Preparedness, Response, and Recovery . In: *Oxford Research Encyclopedia of Natural Hazard Science*. Oxford: Oxford University Press, pp. 1–20. DOI:10.1093/acrefore/9780199389407.013.12.

American Red Cross, 2014. *Disaster Relief*. [Online] Available at: http://www.redcross.org/what-we-do/disaster-relief [Accessed 23 June 2014].

Anderson, W., n.d. Military Organizations in Natural Disaster. *American Behavioral Scientist*, 13(3), pp. 415–422.

Archibugi, D., 2003. Cosmopolitical Democracy. In: D. Archibugi, ed. *Debating Cosmopolitics*. London: Verso, pp. 1–15.

Archibugi, D., 2004. Cosmopolitan Guidelines for Humanitarian Intervention. *Alternatives*, 29(1), pp. 1–21.

Ashford, E., 2003. The Demandingness of Scanlon's Contractualism. *Ethics*, 113(2), pp. 273–302. DOI:10.1086/342853.

Asia-Pacific Centre for the Responsibility to Protect, 2008. *Cyclone Nargis and the Responsibility to Protect*. Brisbane: University of Queensland.

Asian Development Bank, 2008. "Myanmar: An Update on Country Developments" Bangkok. https://reliefweb.int/sites/reliefweb.int/files/resources/6C2572F095BEBA4C8525745D005AE8BD-Full.Report.pdf ;

Associated Press, 2008. "Disaster Fatigue" Blamed for the Drop in Giving. *NBCNews.com*, 19 May.

Assocaition of Southeast Asian Nations, 2009. *A Bridge to Recovery: ASEAN's Response to Cyclone Nargis*. Asean, Jakarta. https://reliefweb.int/sites/reliefweb.int/files/resources/F0DAABD3FD07A7C5492575FB001EC9E1-Full_Report.pdf

Axworthy, L., 2008. Editorial. *Edmonton Journal*, 13 May.

Barber, R., 2009. The Responsibility to Protect the Survivors of Natural Disaster: Cyclone Nargis, a Case Study. *Journal of Conflict & Security Law*, 14(1), pp. 3–34. DOI:10.1093/jcsl/krn026.

Bawden, T., 2014. Flooded Britain: The Police, the Military and the Government: Exactly Who Is in Charge of What? *The Independent*, 12 February.

BBC News, 2016. Syria: The Story of the Conflict. BBC, 3 February. https://www.bbc.co.uk/news/world-middle-east-26116868

BBC Sinhala, 2005. Useless Teddy Bear: Kadirgamar. *BBCSinhala.com*, 17 March.

Beake, N., 2019. Myanmar Rohingya: Aung San Suu Kyi Cuts a Haunted Figure in Court. *BBCNews*, 14 December, pp. 269–282. https://www.bbc.co.uk/news/world-asia-50770961

Beitz, C., 2001. Human Rights as a Common Concern. *American Political Science Review*, 95(2). DOI:10.1017/S0003055401992019

Beitz, C., 2003. What Human Rights Mean. *Daedalus*, 132(1), pp. 36–46.

Belanger, J. & Horsey, R, 2008. *Negotiating Humanitarian Access to Cyclone-Affected Areas of Myanmar: A Review*. London, UK: Humanitarian Practice Network.

Bentham, J., 2002. Nonsense Upon Stilts, or Pandora's Box Opened, or the French Declaration of Rights Prefixed to the Consitution of 1791 Laid Open and Exposed: With a Comparative Sketch of What has Been Done on the Same Subject in the Const of 1795, & a Sample of Citizen. In: P. Schofield, Pease-Watkin, C. & Blamires, C, eds. *Rights, Representation, and Reform: Nonsense Upon Stilts and Other Writings on the French Revolution*. Oxford: Clarendon.

Bernstein, 2002. Marginal Cases and Moral Relevance. *Journal of Social Philosophy*, 33(4), pp. 523–539. DOI:10.3197/096327/109X404753.

Blaikie, P., Wisner, B., Cannon, T. & Davis, I., 2003. *At Risk: Natural Hazards, People's Vulnerability, and Disasters*. 2nd ed. London: Routledge.

Blair, T., 1999. Blair: We Must Act to Save Thousands of Innocent Men, Women and Children. *The Guardian*, 23 March.

Bowley, G. & Erlanger, S., 2008. *Myanmar Faces Pressure to Allow Major Aid Effort. New York Times*, 8 May.

Breau, S.C., 2016. Responses by States. In: S.C. Breau & Samuel, K., eds. *Research Handbook on Disasters and International Law*. Cheltenham: Edward Elgar Publishing Limited, pp. 69–90.

Buis, A., 2020. *How Climate Change May Be Impacting Storms Over Earth's Tropical Oceans*. [Online] Available at: https://climate.nasa.gov/blog/2956/how-climate-change-may-be-impacting-storms-over-earths-tropical-oceans/[Accessed 14 September 2020].

Cabrera, L., 2004. *Political Theory of Global Justice: A Cosmopolitan Case for the World State*. London: Routledge.

Cabrera, L., 2010. *The Practice of Global Citizenship*. Cambridge: Cambridge University Press.

Camus, A., 2008. *Neither Victim Nor Executioner*. Eugene, OR: Wipf and Stock Publisher.

Caney, S., 2009. Cosmopolitanism and Justice. In: *Contemporary Debates in Political Philosophy*. Hoboken, NJ: Wiley-Blackwell, pp. 387–407.

Caney, S., 2010. Climate Change, Human Rights and Moral Thresholds. In: E.A. Gardner, ed. *Climate Ethics*. Oxford: Oxford University Press, pp. 163–180.

Caney, S., 2013. Agents of Global Justice. In: D. Archard, Deveaux, M, Manson, N. & Weinstock, D, eds. *Reading Onora O'Neill*. Oxon: Routledge, pp. 133–156.

Caney, S., 2014. Two Kinds of Climate Justice: Avoiding Harm and Sharing Burdens. *The Journal of Political Philosophy*, 22(2), pp. 125–149. DOI:0.1111/jopp.12030.

Carter, M., Little, P., Mogues, T. & Negatu, W., 2007. Poverty Traps and Natural Disasters in Ethiopia and Honduras. *World Development*, 35(5), pp. 835–856. DOI:10.1016/j.worlddev.2006.09.010.

Case Concerning the Military and Paramilitary Activities in and against Nicaragua. 1986. Reports of Judgements Advisory Opinions and Orders. Military and Paramiliary Activities in and against Nicaragua (Nicaragua v United States). International Court of Justice.

Chappell, T., 2011. On the Very Idea of Criteria for Personhood. *The Southern Journal of Philosophy*, 49(1), pp. 1–27. DOI:10.1111/j.2041-6962.2010.00042.x.

Chopra, J. & Weiss, 1992. "Sovereignty is No Longer Sacrosanct: Codifying Humanitarian Intervention." *Ethics & Internaitonal Affairs*, pp. 95–117.

Clausewitz, C., 1997. *On War*. Ware, Herefordshre: Wordsworth.

Cohen, R., 2008. The Burma Cyclone and the Responsibility to Protect. *Brookings*, 21 July. https://www.brookings.edu/on-the-record/the-burma-cyclone-and-the-responsibility-to-protect/

Conces, R., 2001. Justifying Coercive and Non-Coercive Intervention: Strategic and Humanitarian Arguments. *Acta Analytica*, 16(27), pp. 133–152.

Convery, I., Mort, M., Baxter, J. & Bailey, C., 2008. *Animal Disease and Human Trauma*. London: Palgrave Macmillan.

Cranston, M., 1967. Human Rights, Real and Supposed. In: D.D. Raphael, ed. *Political Theory and the Rights of Man*. London: Macmillan, pp. 43–54.

Crisp, R., 2016. Well-Being. *The Stanford Encyclopedia of Philosophy*. Fall 2017 Edition, Edward N. Zalta (ed.), https://plato.stanford.edu/archives/fall2017/entries/well-being/

Cross, F., 2001. The Error of Positive Rights. *UCLA Law Review*, 48.

Cutter, S. et al., 2008. A Place-Based Model for Understanding Community Resilience to Natural Disasters. *Global Environmental Change*, 18, pp. 598–606. DOI:10.1016/j.gloenvcha.2008.07.013.

Das, R., 2006. Book Review: Political Theory of Global Justice: A Cosmopolitan Case for the World State. *Journal of International Political Theory*, 2(1), pp. 97–100. DOI:10.3366/per.2006.2.1.97.

Deng, F., 2010. From "Sovereignty as Responsibility" to the "Responsibility to Protect". *Global Responsibility to Protect*, 2, pp. 353–370. DOI:10.1163/18759 8410X519534.

DeTorrente, N., 2006. Humanitarian NGOs Must Not Ally with the Military. *European Affairs*. https://www.doctorswithoutborders.org/what-we-do/news-stories/research/humanitarian-ngos-must-not-ally-military

deWijze, S., 2013. Punishing "Dirty Hands": Three Justifications. *Ethical Theory in Moral Practice*, 16, pp. 879–897. DOI:10.1007/s 10677-012-9396-x.

DHS, 2015a. *National Preparedness Goal*. [Online] Available at: https://www.fema.gov/national-preparedness-goal# [Accessed 20 February 2016].

DHS, 2015b. *Whole Community*. [Online] Available at: https://www.fema.gov/whole-community-0 [Accessed 20 February 2016].

Department of Homeland Security/Federal Emergency Management Agency (DHS/FEMA, 2015. *International Assistance System Concept of Operations*. Washington, DC: Federal Emergency Management Agency.

Diamond, C., 2005/2012. Eating Meat and Eating People. In: C. Sunstein & Nussbaum, M, eds. *Animal Rights: Current Debates and New Directions*. Oxford: Oxford Scholarship Online, pp. 93–107.

Dobos, N., 2012. *Insurrection and Intervention: The Two Faces of Sovereignty*. Cambridge: Cambridge University Press. DOI:10.1017/CBO9781139049214.

Doherty, B., 2015. France Launches “Massive” Airstrike on Isis Stronghold of Raqqa. *The Guardian*, 16 November.

Donnelly, J., 2014. State Sovereignty and International Human Rights. *Ethics & International Affairs*, 28(2), pp. 225–238. DOI:10.1017/S0892679414000239.

Doppelt, G., 1978. Walzer’s Theory of Morality in International Relations. *Philosophy & Public Affairs*, 8(1), pp. 3–26.

EMERCOM of Russia, 2017. *EMERCOM*. [Online] Available at: http://en.mchs.ru/ [Accessed 30 April 2017].

Euro-Atlantic Partnership Council, 1998. *EAPC Policy on Enhanced Practical Cooperation in the Field of International Disaster Relief.* Brussels: ECHO.

European Commission, 2011. Cooperation in Disaster Management: The European Union and the United States Take a Major Step Forward. 17 November.

European Commission, 2012. *The EU Approach to Resilience: Learning from Food Security Crises*. European Commission. https://ec.europa.eu/knowledge4policy/publication/eu-approach-resilience-learning-food-security-crises-com2012-586_en#:~:text=23%20November%202018-,The%20EU%20Approach%20to%20Resilience%20%2D%20Learning%20from%20Food,Crises%2DCOM(2012)%20586&text=The%20communication%20entitled%20%22The%20EU,of%20future%20crises%20and%20disasters.

Evans, G., 2008. Facing Up to Our Responsibilities. *The Guardian*, 12 May. https://www.theguardian.com/commentisfree/2008/may/12/facinguptoourresponsbilities

Faiez, R. & Sraziuso, J, 2014. Afghanistan’s Karzai Criticizes US in Farewell Speech, Says America Wants War. *The Globe and Mail*, 23 September. https://www.reuters.com/article/us-afghanistan-karzai-idUSKCN0HI0LY20140923

Fabre, C., 2012. *Cosmopolitan War*. Oxford: Oxford University Press.

Federal Emergency Management Agency (FEMA), 2013. *Natural Disasters*. [Online] Available at: http://www.ready.gov/natural-disasters [Accessed 11 July 2015].

FEMA, 2014. *Disaster Declarations for 2014*, Washington, DC: FEMA.

Fixdal, M. & Smith, D, 1998. Humanitarian Intervention and Just War. *Mershon International Studies Review*, 42, pp. 283–312.

Fletcher, G., 2013. A Fresh Start for the Objective-List Theory of Well-Being. *Utilitas*, 25(2), pp. 206–220.

The Fog of War. 2003. [Film] Directed by E Morris. United States: Sony Classics.

Foot, P., 2002. Killing and Letting Die. In: *Moral Dilemmas: And Other Topics in Moral Philosophy*. Oxford: Oxford Scholarship Online. DOI:10.1093/019925284X.003.0006.

Franklin, J., 2014. Tsunami Warning and Evacuation of Thousands after Earthquake in Chile. *The Guardian*, 2 April. https://www.theguardian.com/world/2014/apr/02/chile-earthquake-sparks-tsunami-warning-and-evacuation-of-thousands

Freiman, C., 2013. Cosmopolitanism Within Borders: On Behalf of Charter Cities. *Journal of Applied Philosophy*, 30(1), pp. 40–52. DOI:10.1111/japp.12008.

Fund for Peace, 2010. *The Failed State Index 2010*. Washington, DC: The Fund for Peace.

Fund for Peace, 2014. *Conflict Assessment Framework Manual*. Washington, DC: The Fund for Peace Publication.

Fund for Peace, 2015a. *What Can Be Done to Avert Further Weakening of States at Risk and to Stimulate Recovery?* Washington, DC.

Fund for Peace, 2015b. *What Does State Fragility Mean?* Washington, DC: Fund for Peace.

Gaus, G., 2003. Dirty Hands. In: R. Frey & Wellman, C.H., eds. *A Companion to Applied Ethics.* Malden, MA: Blackwell, pp. 167–179.

Giddens, A., 2002. *The Nation-State and Violence.* Cambridge: Polity Press.

Griffin, J., 1988/2003. *Well-Being: Its Meaning, Measurement, and Moral Importance.* Oxford: Oxford Scholarship Online. DOI:10.1093/0198248431.001.0001.

Griffin, J., 2000. Welfare Rights. *Journal of Ethics*, 4(1/2), pp. 27–43.

Griffin, J., 2008. *On Human Rights.* Oxford: Oxford University Press.

Haider, H., 2013. *International Legal Frameworks for Humanitarian Action.* Birmingham, UK: GSDRC, University of Birmingham.

Harper, E., 2009. *International Law and Standards Applicable in Natural Disaster Scenarios.* Geneva: International Development Law Organization.

Hasner, M., 1999. Killing, Letting Die and Preventing People from Being Saved. *Utilitas*, 11(3), pp. 277–295.

Heathwood, C., 2006. Desire Satisfactionism and Hedonism. *Philosophical Studies*, 128, pp. 539–563. DOI:10.1007/s11098-004-7817-y.

Henderson, B., 2015. What Have Been the Successes and Failures of UN Peacekeeping Missions? *The Telegraph*, 28 September. https://www.telegraph.co.uk/news/worldnews/europe/bosnia/11729436/Srebrenica-20-years-on-What-have-been-the-successes-and-failures-of-UN-peacekeeping-missions.html

Hofmann, C. & Hudson, L, 2009. *Military Responses to Natural Disasters: Last Resort or Inevitable Trend?* London: Humanitarian Practice Network.

Holzgrefe, J.L., 2003. The Humanitarian Intervention Debate. In: J.L. Holzgrefe & Keohane, R, eds. *Humanitarian Intervention: Ethical, Legal and Political Dilemmas.* Cambridge: Cambridge University Press, pp. 15–52.

Hooker, B., 2000. *Ideal Code, Real World.* Oxford: Clarendon Press.

Human Rights Watch, 1989. *Burma (Myanmar).* New York: HRW.

Interagency standing Committee, 2006. *IASC Operational Guidelines on Human Rights and Natural Disasters.* Washington, DC: Brookings-Bern Project on Internal Displacement.

International Commission on Intervention and State Sovereignty (ICISS), 2001. *Responsibility to Protect.* Ottawa: International Development Research Centre.

International Committee of the Red Cross (ICRC), 1977. *Protocol Additional to the Geneva Conventions of 12 August 1949, and Relating to the Protection of Victims of International Armed Conflicts (Protocol I)*, Geneva: ICRC.

International Committee of the Red Cross (ICRC), 2013. Convention on the Prevention and Punishment of the Crime of Genocide. Geneva: ICRC.

International Federation of the Red Cross (IFRC), 2004. *World Disasters Report 2004: From Risk to Resilience: Helping Communities Cope with Crisis.* Geneva: International Federation of the Red Cross.

IFRC, 2007. *Guidelines for the Domestic Facilitation and Regulation of International Disaster Relief and Initial Recovery Assistance* (IDRL Guidelines). Geneva: IFRC.

IFRC, 2011. *Myanmar: Cyclone Nargis 2008 Facts and Figures.* Geneva: IFRC. https://www.ifrc.org/en/news-and-media/news-stories/asia-pacific/myanmar/myanmar-cyclone-nargis-2008-facts-and-figures/

IFRC, 2016. *World Disasters Report.* Geneva: IFRC.

IFRC, 2017. *Promoting the Fundamental Principles and Humanitarian Values.* [Online] Available at: http://www.ifrc.org/en/who-we-are/vision-and-mission/principles-and-values/ [Accessed 24 June 2017].

Ignatieff, M., 2000. *Human Rights as Politics.* Princeton, NJ: The Tanner Lectures on Human Values.

IMF (International Monetary Fund) Survey, 2012. *Natural Disasters Hitting More People, Becoming More Costly.* Japan: International Monetary Fund.

INSARAG), 2011. *The INSARAG Asia-Pacific Exercise in Chengdu, China.* [Online] Available at: http://www.insarag.org/en/regional-groups/asia-pacific/exercises-asia-pasific/85-group-meeting-1-2010.html [Accessed 1 February 2015].

INSARAG, 2013. *Regional Exercises 2013.* [Online] Available at: http://www.insarag.org/en/regional-groups/americas/exercises-americas/245-regional-exercise-2013.html [Accessed 1 February 2015].

Intergovernmental Panel on Climate Change, 2013. *Working Group 1 Contribution to the IPCC Fifth Assessment Report (AR5), Climate Change 2013: The Physical Science Basis.* Stockholm: Working Group 1 – Twelfth Session.

International Coalition for the Responsibility to Protect, 2008. Responsibility to Protect: Engaging Civil Society. [Online] Available at: http://responsibilitytoprotect.org/index.php/component/content/article/1653 [Accessed 9 October 2013].

International Criminal Court, 1998. Rome Statue of the International Criminal Court. Rome: United Nations, Treaty Series vol 2187, No. 38544, Depositary: Secretary-General of the United Nations.

International Criminal Court, 2002. The Rome Statute of the International Criminal Court. Rome: The United Nations Diplomatic Conference of Plenipotentiaries on the Establishment of an International Criminal Court.

International Law Commission, 2001/2008. *Draft Articles on Responsibility of States for Internationally Wrongful Acts.* ILC.

International Search and Rescue Advisory Group, 2011. *Guidelines and Methodology.* United Nations Office for the Coordination of Humanitarian Affairs

International Strategy for Disaster Reduction, 2008. 2008–2009 ISDR System Joint Work Programme. Geneva: United Nations.

IRIN News, 2009. How to Do a Food Airdrop. *Irin News*, 30 July. https://www.thenewhumanitarian.org/feature/2009/07/30/how-do-food-airdrop

Iser, M., 2013. Recognition. *The Stanford Encyclopedia of Philosophy.* https://plato.stanford.edu/search/r?entry=/entries/recognition/&page=1&total_hits=697&pagesize=10&archive=None&rank=0&query=recognition

James, A., 1986. *Sovereign Statehood.* London: Allan & Unwin. DOI:10.1177/004711788700900111.

JF, 2016. "Should say Myanmar or Burma?" The Economist. 20 December, https://www.economist.com/the-economist-explains/2016/12/20/should-you-say-myanmar-or-burma. Accessed 12 Nov 2020.

Johnson, J., 1984. *Can Modern War Be Just.* New Haven: Yale University Press. DOI:10.1177/004057368604300118.

Kaldor, M., 2010. *New and Old Wars.* 2nd ed. Cambridge: Polity Press.

Kelly, M., 2014. Introduction. In: D. Caron, Kelly, M. & Telesetsky, A., eds. *The International Law of Disaster Relief.* Cambridge: Cambridge University Press, pp. 1–6.

Kelman, I., 2008. *Disaster Lexicon.* http://www.ilankelman.org/miscellany.html

Kelman, I., 2018. Lost for Words Amongst Disaster Risk Science Vocabulary? *International Journal of Disaster Risk Science*, 9, pp. 281–291. DOI:10.1007/s13753-018-0188-3.

Kelman, I., 2019. Axioms and Actions for Preventing Disasters. *Progress in Disaster Science*, 2, pp. 1-3. DOI:10.1016/j.pdisas.2019.100008.

Kelman, I., Gaillard, C., Lewis, J. & Mercer, J., 2016. Learning from the History of Disaster Vulnerability and Resilience Research and Practice for Climate Change. *Natural Hazards*, 82, pp. 129–143. DOI:10.1007/s11069-016-2294-0.

Kelman, I, Mercer, J. & Gaillard, J.C., 2017. *The Routledge Handbook of Disaster Risk Reduction Including Climate Change Adaptation.* 1st ed. London: Routledge.

Keylor, W., 2001. *The Twentieth-Century World: An Internaitonal History.* 4th ed. New York: Oxford University Press.

Kiesling, E., 2001. On War Without the Fog. *Military Review*, September–October 2001, pp. 85–87.

Krehoff, B., 2008. Legitimate Political Authority and Sovereignty: Why States Cannot be the Whole Story. *Res Publica,* 14, pp. 283–297. DOI:10.1007/s11158-008-9073-z.

Lauta, K., 2016. Human Rights and Natural Disasters. In: S. Breau & Samuel, K.L.H., eds. *Research Handbook on Disasters and International Law.* Cheltenham: Edward Elgar Publishing, pp. 91–110.

Lewis, J., 2010. *Corruption: The Hidden Perpetrator of Under-Development and Vulnerability to Natural Hazards and Disasters.* Potchefstroom, South Africa: African Centre for Disaster Studies.

Lloyd, S. & Sreedhar, S., 2014. "Hobbes's Moral and Political Philosophy." *The Stanford Encylopeida of Philosophy,* Volume Spring 2014.

Luban, D., 1980. Just War and Human Rights. *Philosophy & Public Affairs*, 9(2), pp. 160–181.

MacKinnon, I., 2009. Burmese Regime Blocked International Aid to Cyclone Victims, Report Says. *The Guardian*, 27 February. https://www.theguardian.com/world/2009/feb/27/regime-blocked-aid-to-burma-cyclone-victims

Maslow, A., 1943. A Theory of Human Motivation. *Psychological Review*, 50(4), pp. 370–396.

Massingham, E., 2009. Military Intevention for Humanitarian Purposes: Does the Responsibility to Protect Doctrine Advance the Legality of the Use of Force for Humanitarian Ends?. *International Review of the Red Cross*, 91(876), pp. 803–832. DOI:10.1.17/S1816383110000068.

Matthews, M., n.d. *The Posse Comitatus Act and the United States Army: A Historical Perspective.* Fort Leavenworth, KS: Combat Studies Institute Press.

McMahan, J., 2006. Just Cause for War. *Ethics & International Affairs*, 19(3), pp. 1–21. DOI:10.1111/j.1747-7093.2005.tb00551.x.

Miller, D., 2005. Against Global Egalitarianism. In: G. Brock & Moellendorf, D., eds. *Current Debates in Global Justice.* Dordrecht: Springer, pp. 54–79. DOI:10.1007/1-4020-3847-X.

Moellendorf, 2002. *Cosmopolitan Justice.* Cambridge, MA: Westview Press.

Morris, C., 1998. Sovereignty. In: *An Essay on the Modern State.* Cambridge: Cambridge University Press, pp. 172–227.

Morris, C., 2000. The Very Idea of Popular Sovereignty: "We the People" Reconsidered. Social Philosophy & Policy Foundation, pp. 1–26.

Moss, J., 2013. The Foundations of Well-Being. *The Australian Economic Review*, 46(1), pp. 62–69. DOI:10.1111/j.1467-8462.2013.12001.x.

Multinational, 2007. *Guidelines on the Use of Foreign Military and Civil Defence Assets in Disaster Relief.* Oslo: Office for the Coordination of Humanitarian Affairs.

Mydans, S., 2008. Myanmar Faces Pressure to Allow Major Aid Effort. *The New York Times*, 8 May. https://www.nytimes.com/2008/05/08/world/asia/08myanmar.html

Nardin, T., 2005. Response to "Ending Tyranny in Iraq": Humanitarian Imperialism. *Ethics & International Affairs*, 19(2), pp. 21–26.

NASA, 2020. *Climate Change: How Do We Know?* [Online] Available at: https://climate.nasa.gov/evidence/ [Accessed 14 September 2020].

National Disaster Coordinating Council (Phillippines), 2010. *Implementing Rules and Regulations of Republic Act No. 10121.* Manila: Phillippines National Defense.

National Geographic, 2015. *Natural Disasters.* [Online] Available at: http://environment.nationalgeographic.com/environment/natural-disasters/ [Accessed 11 July 2015].

NATO, 1998. *EAPC Policy on Enhanced Practical Cooperation in the Field of International Disaster Relief.* Brussels: North Atlantic Treaty Organisation.

Neal, D., 1997. Reconsidering the Phases of Disaster. *International Journal of Mass Emergencies and Disasters*, 15(2), pp. 239–264.

Nickel, J., 1987. *Making Sense of Human Rights.* 1st ed. Berkeley and Los Angeles: University of California Press.

Nickel, J., 2013. *Making Sense of Human Rights.* 2nd ed. Malden, MA: Blackwell.

Nickel, J., 2017. Human Rights. In: E. Zalta, ed. *The Stanford Encylopedia of Philosophy.* Summer 2019 Edition, Edward N. Zalta (ed.), https://plato.stanford.edu/archives/sum2019/entries/rights-human/

NobelPrize.org, 1991. *Aung San Suu Kyi: Facts.* [Online] Available at: https://www.nobelprize.org/prizes/peace/1991/summary/ [Accessed 15 September 2020].

Nussbaum, M., 1997. Capabilities and Human Rights. *Fordham Law Review*, 66(2), pp. 273–300.

Nussbaum, M., 1999. Women and Equality: The Capabilities Approach. *International Labour Review*, 138(3), pp. 227–245. DOI:10.1111/j.1564-913X.1999.tb00386.x.

Nussbaum, M., 2001. Symposium on Amartya Sen's Philosophy: five Adaptive Preferences and Women's Options. *Economics and Philosophy*, 17, pp. 67–88. DOI:10.1017/S0266267101000153.

Nussbaum, M., 2007a. Beyond the Social Contract: Capabilities and Global Justice. *Oxford Development Studies*, pp. 3–18. DOI:10.1080/1360081042000184093.

Nussbaum, M., 2007b. Human Rights and Human Capabilities. *Harvard Human Rights Journal*, 20, pp. 21–24.

Nussbaum, M., 2011. *Creating Capabilities: The Human Development Approach.* Cambridge, MA: The Belknap Press of Harvard University Press.

OCHA, 2004. *Guiding Principles of Internal Displacement.* New York: United Nations.

OCHA, 2017. *ReliefWeb.* [Online] Available at: http://reliefweb.int/ [Accessed 3 June 2017].

O'Donnell, T. &. Allan, C., 2016. A Duty of Solidarity? The International Law Commission's Draft Articles and the Right to Offer Assistance in Disasters. In:

S.C. Breau & K.L. Samuel, ed. *Research Handbook on Disasters and International Law*. Cheltenham: Edward Elgar Publishing Limited, pp. 453–474.

Office of the Press Secretary, 2006. The Security and Prosperity Partnership of North America: Next Steps. *White House Press Release*, 31 March. https://2001-2009.state.gov/p/wha/rls/prsrl/2006/q1/69852.htm

OHCHR, 2017. *Key Concepts on ESCRs: What Are Examples of Violations of Economic, Social and Cultural Rights?* Geneva: Office of the United Nations High Commissioner for Human Rights.

O'Mathuna, D., 2014. Disasters. In ten Have H., Gordijn B. (eds) Handbook of Global Bioethics. Springer, Dordrecht, pp. 619-639. DOI: 10.1007/978-94-007-2512-6_107.

Omelicheva, M., 2011. Natural Disasters: Triggers of Political Instability. *International Interactions*, 37(4), pp. 44–465. DOI:10.1080/03050629.2011.622653.

Orend, B., 2008. *War*. The Stanford Encyclopedia of Philosophy. Fall 2008 Edition, Edward N. Zalta (ed.), https://plato.stanford.edu/archives/fall2008/entries/war/.

Otsuka, M., 1998. Incompatibilism and the Avoidability of Blame. *Ethics*, 108(4), pp. 685–701. DOI:10.1086/233847.

Ozerdem, A., 2010. The "Responsibility to Protect" in Natural Disasters: Another Excuse for Interventionism? Nargis Cyclone in Myanmar. *Conflict, Security & Development*, 10(5), pp. 693–713. DOI:10.1080/14678802.2010.511511.

Peace, R., 2010. Winning Hearts and Minds: The Debate Over US Intervention in Nicaragua in the 1980s. *Peace & Change*, 35(1), pp. 1–38. DOI:10.1111/j.1468-0130.2009.00611.x.

Peter, F., 2010. Political Legitimacy. *The Stanford Encyclopedia of Philosophy*. Summer 2017 Edition, Edward N. Zalta (ed.), https://plato.stanford.edu/archives/sum2017/entries/legitimacy/

Philpott, D., 2010. *Sovereignty*. [Online] Available at: http://plato.stanford.edu/entries/sovereignty/#1 [Accessed 28 August 2013].

Pogge, T., 1992. Cosmopolitanism and Sovereignty. *Ethics*, 103(1), pp. 48–75.

Pogge, T., 2002. Cosmopolitanism: A Defence. *CRISPP*, 5(3), pp. 86–81. DOI:10.1080/13698230410001702672.

Pogge, T., 2001. Priorities of Global Justice. *Metaphilosophy*, 32(1/2), pp. 6–24.

Pogge, T., 2008. *World Poverty and Human Rights: Cosmopolitan Responsibilities and Reforms*. 2nd ed. Cambridge: Polity Press.

Pogge, T., 2011. Are We Violating the Rights of the World's Poor? *Yale Human Rights & Development Law Journal*, 14(2), pp. 1–33.

PreventionWeb, 2015. *Intensive and Extensive Risk*. [Online] Available at: http://www.preventionweb.net/risk/intensive-extensive-risk [Accessed 24 June 2017].

Protezione Civile, 2017. Protezione Civile. [Online] Available at: http://www.protezionecivile.gov.it/jcms/en/home.wp;jsessionid=760AB797A289E79EE0E75D42026F11E2.worker2 [Accessed 30 April 2017].

Quarantelli, E.L., 1998. Epilogue: Where We Have Been and Where We Might Go. In: E. L. Quarantelli, ed. *What Is a Disaster? Perspectives on the Question*. London: Routledge, pp. 234–273.

Quarantelli, E.L., 2000. *Disaster Planning, Emergency Management and Civil Protection: The Historical Development of Organized Efforts to Plan for and to Respond to Disasters*. University of Deleware Disaster Research Paper. Newark, Deleware: Disaster Research Center.

Quarantelli, E.L. & Dynes, R, 1973. When Disaster Strikes. *New Society*, 23, pp. 5–9.

Quarantelli, E.L. & Dynes, R., 1977. Response to Social Crisis and Disaster. *Annual Review of Sociology*, 3, pp. 23–49.

Raz, J., 1985. Authority and Justification. *Philosophy & Public Affairs*, 14(1), pp. 3–29.

Record, J., 2003. The Bush Doctrine and War with Iraq. *Parameters*, 33, pp. 1–21.

Reuters, 2008. Factbox: Sierra Leone's Civil War. *Reuters.com*, 8 January.

RT, 2015. 6.0 Magnitude Earthquake Hits Near Peru-Chile Border. Reuters, 23 March. http://www.rt.com/news/243101-quake-powerful-peru-tacna/. Accessed 27 July 2015.

Reuters Staff, 2009. FACTBOX-Key Facts About Cyclone Nargis, *Reuters News.* 30 April. https://uk.reuters.com/article/idUSSP420097

Rice, C., 2013. Defending the Objective List Theory of Well-Being. *Ratio*, 26, pp. 196–211. DOI:10.1111/rati.12007.

Robinson, C., 2007. Humanitarian Intervention, Dirty Hands, and Deliberation. *Central European Journal of International & Security Studies*, 1(1), pp. 85–100.

Ronzoni, M., 2013. For (Some) Political and Insitutional Cosmopolitanism, (even if) Against Moral Cosmopolitanism. In: G. Brock, ed. *Cosmopolitanism versus Non-Cosmopolitanism: Critiques, Defenses, Reconceptualizations.* Oxford: Oxford Scholarship Online, pp. 156–174.

Rousseau, J., 1998. *The Social Contract.* Ware: Wordsworth Editions Limited.

Sartre, J., 1948. *Dirty Hands.*

Schilde, K., 2015. War Powers, Private Actors, and National Security State Capacity. *Boston University Law Review*, 95, pp. 1369–1385.

Sen, A., 1985. Well-Being, Agency and Freedom: The Dewey Lectures 1984. *Journal of Philosophy*, 82(4), pp. 169–221. DOI:10.2307/2026184.

Sen, A., 1993. Capability and Well-Being. In: M. Nussbaum & Sen, A, eds. *The Quality of Life.* Oxford: Clarendon Press, pp. 30–66. DOI:10.1093/0198287976.003.0003.

Sen, A., 1999. *Development as Freedom.* Oxford: Oxford University Press.

Shafer-Landau, R., 2012. *The Fundamentals of Ethics.* 2nd ed. New York: Oxford University Press.

Shea, J., 2016. *Resilience: A Core Element of Collective Defence.* Brussels: NATO Review.

Shue, H., 1980. *Basic Rights: Subsistence, Affluence, and US Foreign Policy.* Princeton, NJ: Princeton University Press.

Singer, P., 1972. Famine, Affluence and Morality. *Philosophy & Public Affairs*, 1(3), pp. 229–243.

Singer, P., 2003. Animal Liberation at 30. *The New York Review of Books*, 50(8). https://www.nybooks.com/articles/2003/05/15/animal-liberation-at-30/

Sinnott-Armstrong, W., 2015. Consequentialism. *The Stanford Encyclopedia of Philosophy*, Summer 2019 Edition, Edward N. Zalta (ed.). https://plato.stanford.edu/archives/sum2019/entries/consequentialism/

Soucy, J., 2012. Guard's Role in Disaster Response Defined More Clearly. US Army, 3 March. https://www.army.mil/article/74990/guards_role_in_disaster_response_defined_more_clearly

Spencer, R., 2014. Iraq Crisis: The Streets of Erbil's Newly Christian Suburb Are Now Full of Helpless People. *The Telegraph*, 8 August. https://www.telegraph

.co.uk/news/worldnews/middleeast/iraq/11022879/Iraq-crisis-The-streets-of-Erbils-newly-Christian-suburb-are-now-full-of-helpless-people.html

Squires, N., 2009. Italy Earthquake: L'Aquila One Month on. *The Telegraph*, 2 May. https://www.telegraph.co.uk/news/worldnews/europe/italy/5262449/Italy-earthquake-LAquila-one-month-on.html

Stanulova, M., 2010. *Has Humanitarian Intervention Become an Exception to the Prohibition on the Use of Force in Article 2(4) of the UN Charter*. Edinburgh: University of Edinburgh.

Stevenson, D., 2001. *The First World War and International Politics*. Oxford: Oxford University Press.

Stuhltrager, J., 2006. Send in the Guard: The National Guard Response to Natural Disasters. *Natural Resources & Environment*, 20(4), pp. 21–25.

Survival, 2014. *The Uncontacted Indians of Brazil*. [Online] Available at: http://www.survivalinternational.org/tribes/uncontacted-brazil [Accessed 9 May 2014].

Tesón, F., 2004. The Liberal Case for Humanitarian Intervention. In: J. Holzgrefe & Keohane, R, eds. *Humanitarian Intervention: Ethical, Legal and Political Dilemmas*. Cambridge: Cambridge University Press, pp. 93–129. DOI:10.1017/CBO9780511494000.004.

Thakur, R., 2008. Should the UN Invoke the "Responsibility to Protect"? *The Globe and Mail*, 8 May.

The Economist, 2013. Where Did the Banana Republics Get Their Name? *The Economist*, 21 November. https://www.economist.com/the-economist-explains/2013/11/21/where-did-banana-republics-get-their-name

Thomson, J.J., 1976. Killing, Letting Die and the Trolley Problem. *The Monist*, 59(2), pp. 204–217.

Tokunaga, E., 2014. Evolution of International Disaster Response Law. In: D. Caron, Kelly, M. & Telesetsky, A., eds. *The International Law of Disaster Relief*. Cambridge: Cambridge University Press, pp. 46–64.

Tolin, L., 2008. "Disaster Fatigue" Leads to Drop in Giving. *Huffington Post*, 30 July.

UNGA (United Nations General Assembly), 1991. *Strengthening of the Coordination of Humanitarian Emergency Assistance of the United Nations*. New York: United Nations.

UNGA, 2005. *2005* World Summit Outcome. New York: UNGA.

UNGA, 2009. *Implementing the Responsibility to Protect*. New York: UNGA.

UNGA, 2014. *Suggested Elements for the Post-2015 Framework for Disaster Risk Reduction*. Geneva: Third United Nations World Conference on Disaster Risk Reduction.

UNGA Economic and Social Council, 2003. *Strengthening of the Coordination of Emergency Humanitarian Assistance of the United Nations*. Geneva: UNGA.

United Nations, 2008. *Myanmar Tropical Clyclone Nargis Flash Appeal*. New York: OCHA. https://www.iom.int/jahia/webdav/shared/shared/mainsite/media/docs/reports/myanma_flash_appeal%202008.pdf

United Nations Office for Disaster Risk Reduction, 2015. *Sendai Framework for Disaster Risk Reduction*. Sendai, Japan: United Nations Office for Disaster Risk Reduction .

UNISDR, 2017. *What is Disaster Risk Reduction?* Geneva, Switzerland: UNISDR. https://www.unisdr.org/files/7817_UNISDRTerminologyEnglish.pdf

United Nations, 1948. *The Universal Declaration of Human Rights.* New York: United Nations.

United Nations, 1976. *International Covenant on Civil and Political Rights.* New York: United Nations Office of the High Commissioner for Human Rights.

United Nations, 2006. Burundi – ONUB – *Background.* Geneva: United Nations.

United Nations, 2013a. *Democracy and the United Nations.* [Online] Available at: http://www.un.org/en/events/democracyday/pdf/presskit.pdf [Accessed 14 August 2103].

United Nations, 2013b. *Haiti Humanitarian Action Plan.* New York: UNOCHA.

United Nations, 2015a. *Charter of the United Nations.* Geneva: United Nations.

United Nations, 2015b. *Principles of UN Peacekeeping.* [Online] Available at: http://www.un.org/en/peacekeeping/operations/principles.shtml#noforce [Accessed 7 February 2015].

United Nations, 2016. *Draft Articles on the Protection of Persons in the Event of Disasters*, New York: United Nations.

United Nations Enable, 2004. *International Norms and Standards Relating to Disability.* New York: Department of Economic and Social Affairs.

UNOCHA, 2014. *Humanitarian Access.* [Online] Available at: http://www.unocha.org/what-we-do/policy/thematic-areas/humanitarian-access [Accessed 11 August 2014].

United States Holocaust Memorial Museum, n.d. *The Genocide Convention in International Law.* [Online] Available at: http://www.ushmm.org/confront-genocide/justice-and-accountability/introduction-to-the-definition-of-genocide [Accessed 2 November 2014].

Valentini, L., 2012. Human Rights, Freedom and Political Authority. *Political Theory*, 40(5), pp. 573–601. DOI:10.1177/0090591712451721.

Van Parijs, P., 2004. Equality of Resources v Undominated Diversity. In: J. Burley, ed. *Dworkin and His Critics: With Replies by Dworkin.* Malden, MA: Blackwell, pp. 45–69.

Voltaire, 1918. *Candide.* New York: Boni & Liveright.

Waldron, J., 1987. Nonsense Upon Stilts?: A Reply. In: J. Waldron, ed. *Nonsense Upon Stilts: Bentham, Burke and Marx on the Rights of Man.* New York: Methuen, pp. 151–209.

Wallechinsky, D., 2011. What Is the Real Reason George Bush Invaded Iraq?. *Huffington Post*, 25 May. https://www.huffingtonpost.com/david-wallechinsky/what-is-the-real-reason-g_b_11116.html?ncid=engmodushpmg00000004

Walzer, M., 1980. The Moral Standing of States: A Response to Four Critics. *Philosophy & Public Affairs*, 9(3), pp. 209–229.

Walzer, M., 1990. *The Civil Society Argument.* Gunnar Myrdal Lecture. Stockholm: University of Stockholm, S.N, pp. 1-11.

Walzer, M., 1995. The Politics of Rescue. *Social Research*, 62(1), pp. 53–66.

Walzer, M., 2002. The Argument About Humanitarian Intervention. *Dissent*, 49(1).

Walzer, M., 2004a. Emergency Ethics. In: *Arguing About War.* New Haven: Yale University Press, pp. 33–51.

Walzer, M., 2004b. Political Action: The Problem of Dirty Hands. In: S. Levinson, ed. *Torture: A Collection.* Oxford:Oxford University Press, pp. 68–83.

Walzer, M., 2006a. *Just & Unjust Wars.* 4th ed. New York: Basic Books.

Walzer, M., 2006b. *Just and Unjust Wars: A Moral Argument with Historical Illustrations.* New York: Basic Books.

Wheeler, N., 2005. *A Victory for Common Humanity? The Responsibility to Protect After the 2005 World Summit.* Toronto, ON: Faculty of Law, University of Toronto.

Wheeler, N., 2010. *Saving Strangers: Humanitarian Intervention in International Society.* Oxford: Oxford University Press. DOI:10.1093/0199253102.001.0001.

Wiharta, S. et al., 2005. *The Effectiveness of Foreign Military Assets in Natural Disaster Response.* Stockholm: SIPRI.

Williams, B., 1991. A Critique of Utilitarianism. In: *Utilitarianism: For & Against.* New York: Press Syndicate of the University of Cambridge, pp. 77–150.

Williams, C., 2015. UN Reports Nearly 8000 Deaths in Ukraine War, Laments Russian Role. *Los Angeles Times*, 8 September.

Woolf, N., 2015. Former Blackwater Guards Sentenced for Massacre of Unarmed Iraqi Civilians. *The Guardian*, 13 April. https://www.theguardian.com/us-news/2015/apr/13/former-blackwater-guards-sentencing-baghdad-massacre

Woollard, F., 2012. The Doctrine of Doing and Allowing 1: Analysis of the Doing/Allowing Distinction. *Philosophy Compass*, 7(7), pp. 448–458. DOI:10.1111/j.1747-9991.2012.00491.x.

World Economic Forum, 2008. *Building Resilience to Natural Disasters: A Framework for Private Sector Engagement.* Cologne and Geneva: World Economic Forum, World Bank, UNISDR.

Zack, N., 2011. *Ethics for Disaster.* Plymouth, UK: Rowman & Littlefield.

Index

For Product Safety Concerns and Information please contact our EU
representative GPSR@taylorandfrancis.com
Taylor & Francis Verlag GmbH, Kaufingerstraße 24, 80331 München, Germany

www.ingramcontent.com/pod-product-compliance
Ingram Content Group UK Ltd.
Pitfield, Milton Keynes, MK11 3LW, UK
UKHW022122190926
475702UK00013B/1591
9780367409128